THE

# NEGRO AND THE WHITE MAN.

BY

BISHOP W. J. GAINES, D.D.

Of Georgia.

NEGRO UNIVERSITIES PRESS

NEW YORK

E
185.6
G 14
1969

Originally published in 1897
by the A.M.E. Publishing House

Reprinted 1969 by
Negro Universities Press
A DIVISION OF GREENWOOD PUBLISHING CORP.
NEW YORK

SBN 8371-1889-1

PRINTED IN UNITED STATES OF AMERICA

TO

MY WIFE,

JULIA A. GAINES,

AND ALSO MY DAUGHTER,

MARY L. GAINES,

WHOSE CONSTANT DEVOTION TO ME

AS HUSBAND AND FATHER

HAS COMFORTED AND CHEERED ME THROUGH THE TOILS

OF A METHODIST PREACHER'S LIFE,

THESE PAGES

ARE AFFECTIONATELY DEDICATED.

# CONTENTS.

# INTRODUCTION.

I T has been my purpose for years to put my views on the so-called "Negro Question" into permanent form. The cares and duties of my official life, involving a heavy tax upon my time and strength, have prevented the earlier fulfillment of this cherished purpose. I could not afford, however, at my time of life, to further delay the execution of the work I had mapped out. In the intervals of my Episcopal visits to the conferences and churches I have devoted such time as I had to the preparation of these chapters, which now, for the first time, go forth to the public.

So far as I know, I am the first of my race to take up and discuss in a systematic form this question in all its aspects and phases. It has required research and laborious effort. I have availed myself of such authorities as furnished me with the necessary data for the work, and have endeavored to state correctly all facts which I have used impartially and fairly.

I have striven to divest myself of all prejudice and bias, and to discuss the great question with honesty, candor and, above all, with a purpose to accomplished good. I have no resentments to indulge, no race prejudices to ventilate, no animosities to gratify. I have endeavored to be conservative, and if, in some instances, I have been bold in

7

the statement of my views, it has been with no purpose to wound or irritate. In the language of Dr. Samuel Johnson: "I would write down nothing which, in dying, I would wish to blot." I would close, rather than widen, the breach, if any there be, between the races. I would lift my voice always for harmony on the lines of justice and righteousness, as God has ordained them to exist between man and man. I deem him an enemy to his race, be he white or colored, who foments strife, who seeks to breed discontent, division and hatred. No question can be settled finally and permanently, until it is settled right.

I would reach the great heart of my brother in white. I would assure him that I feel nothing but the sentiment of kindness toward him, and that I recognize that the destiny of the American negro is bound up for weal or woe with his destiny.

I would, in these pages, reach the heart and conscience of my own race, and help them to broader views, better living and nobler aspirations. If, in this desire I should fail, I would feel that my labor had been in vain.

I invoke the charitable criticism of all who may chance to read these pages. I cannot expect all to agree with me in the views I have expressed, or in the conclusions I have reached. But feeling that I have honestly sought to find the truth and to manfully and fearlessly, yet kindly and charitably, give it expression, I send this volume out to the world, earnestly praying that it may be a means of blessing to men.

# CHAPTER I.

THE word "negro" is of Latin origin, derived from *niger*, which means black. It is applied to the races of the African continent, and to their descendants in the Old and New world.

The Egyptians, Berbers, Abyssinians, and Nubians of Northern Africa are not classed as the negro, though there is a strong admixture of negro blood in most of these. The term negro is not a national appellation, but is applied generally to about one-half of the population of Africa, including the most fertile portion of that continent.

Prof. Willis Boughton, of the Ohio University, in an ably written article, which appeared in the *Arena* of September, 1896, says:

"The black race has a history. In fact, all history is full of traces of the black element. It is now usually recognized as the oldest race of which we have any knowledge. The wanderings of these people, since prehistoric history began, have not been confined to the African continent. In Paleolithic times the black man roamed at will over all the fairest portions of the Old World. Europe, as well as Asia and Africa, acknowledges

9

his sway. No white man had as yet appeared to dispute his authority in the vine-clad valleys of France or Germany, or upon the classic hills of Greece or Rome. The black man preceded all others, and carried Paleolithic culture to its very height. But the history of all lands has been only a record of succeeding races. Old races have often been supplanted by those of inferior culture, but of superior energy. More often, however, by fusion of different racial types, and by the mingling of various tribes and peoples, have been evolved new races, superior to any of the original types.

"The blacks were a fundamental element in the origin, not only of the primitive races of Southern Europe, but of the civilized races of antiquity as well. History may be said to begin in ancient Egypt, and recede into the dim past, just as far as records and inscriptions lend us light. Still in the Nile valley we find a civilization that has drawn from all succeeding ages expressions of wonder and admiration. Surely these ancient Egyptians were a remarkable people; but who were they? The ruling tribes are called Hamites—the sunburnt family, according to Dr. Winchell; of Nigritic origin, says Canon Rawlinson. But back of these ruling Hamites were a light-headed people— gay, good-natured, pleasant, sportive, witty, droll, amorous—such are the descriptive terms used in telling the story of these primitive tribes, who, Dr. Taylor says, lived peaceably in those regions for two thousand years before the advent of the Asiatic invaders. Suggestive as they may seem, such terms are truly descriptive of the inhabitants whom we would expect to find in the Nile valley in ancient times. They were probably as purely Nigritic as are the great mass of our own Africo-Americans.

" When the Hamites and their children were at the height of their power, their influence extended to far greater limits than is ordinarily supposed. They pressed toward the confines of Europe, they entered and took possession of the land. 'The Iberians,' says Dr. Winchell (*North American Review*), 'entered by the pillars of Hercules. They came from Northern Africa, at a time when the Hamitic Berbers were gaining possession. They overran the Spanish peninsula, founded cities, built a navy, carried on commerce, extended their empire over Italy, as Sicanes, when Rome was founded, long before the sack of Troy, and from Italy passed into Sicily.' The Pelasgic empire was at its meridian as early as 2500 B.C. This people came from the islands of the Ægian, and more remotely from Asia Minor. They were originally a branch of the sun-burnt Hamitic stock, that laid the basis of civilization in Canaan and Mesopotamia, destined later to be Semitized. Rome itself was Pelasgian to 428 B.C. But in Greece and Italy the Hamitic stock was displaced by Aryan, as in Asia it had been by Semitic.

"The Hellenes were the Aryans first to be brought into contact with these sun-burnt Hamites, who, let it be remembered, though classed as whites, were probably as strongly Negritic as are the Afro-Americans. These Hellenes were savages or barbarians. But Aryan strength and energy were thus brought into contact with Hamitic culture. Then occurred that great struggle of centuries for social equality between the blond Aryan and the Pelasgian, the dark child of the soil. Had it not been for that mixture of dark blood in the Greek composition, that race of poets, artists, and philosophers would never have existed."

Thus it is shown that the negro has figured conspicuously in the earlier history of the world, that his blood entered strongly into that of the conquering Roman and the cultured Greek; that even long before Rome was built or Greece flourished, the descendants of Ham in Egypt had given to the world the highest form of civilization it had then known.

How incredible then is it there should be found any who deny to the negro the possibility of high development. For two thousand years, under the repressive conditions of savage life in dark Africa, it is true that he has made but little progress, but this does not show the want of racial capacity for evolution. Who could have foreseen the virile power and strength of the Aryan race? For thousands of years that race was as ignorant and barbarous as the African in the jungles of his native land, but when at length the proper conditions for its development were furnished by Providence, he sprang into splendid development and has since led his fellows in the race of progress and civilization.

When, in the order of God, the same favorable conditions and environments shall be supplied to the descendants of Ham, they too shall respond to the opportunities offered and develop into a gradually progressive race, worthy to stand shoulder to shoulder with their white brothers on any field of enterprise and achievement.

# CHAPTER II.

## SLAVERY.

AFRICAN slavery was comparatively a modern institution. Slavery, in some form, has existed from the earliest times of which history gives any record. In the first ages of Greece, before Homer sang or Hesiod wrote, it was already fully established. All the Grecian communities were a slave-holding people. In Athens, Corinth and Sparta the slaves constituted a large portion of the population.

The slaves of that day, however, were not negroes, except as now and then a Nubian or an Ethiopian was captured and sold into slavery, but they were whites, chiefly Thracians, Asiatics and even native Greeks. The sources through which the supply was furnished, were captures in wars, piracy, kidnapping and commerce through a systematic slave trade.

The Romans, according to Blair, were the leaders among the ancient peoples in extending the operations and methodizing the details of slavery. The patricians, who were the wealthy and ruling classes, owned thousands of slaves, whom they reduced to absolute serfdom. They were brought mainly from Spain and Gaul and Asiatic countries. So numerous did they become in Italy that the proportion of slaves to freemen was as three to one. "The entire number of slaves would thus have been in the reign of Claudius, 20,832,000; that of the free population being 6,944,000."— *Encyclopedia Britannica.*

No single force, perhaps, contributed more to the final fall and dismemberment of the Roman Empire than slavery. To this evil may be ascribed the degeneracy of the ruling classes who, through the luxury and idleness begotten of it, became sensual and effeminate, and lost that aggressive and warlike spirit which made Rome the mistress of the world.

With the rise of Christianity to controlling influence in the Roman commonwealth the institution began to wane. The Church protested against the multiplication of slaves and everywhere encouraged emancipation. The humanizing influences of religion were arrayed against the cruelty of man enslaving man, and the enlightened sentiment, wrought through a growing Christianity, worked its slow but final death. Theodosius and Justinian began the legislation which looked to the manumission of all slaves and incorporated laws into the Roman code which finally led to the overthrow of this great evil.

It is not the design of these pages to deal at

length with the general history of slavery. It will be enough to say in this connection, that the slaves of the ancient world and of medieval times were chiefly whites, the negro constituting but a small proportion of the immense multitudes who pined and perished amid the cruelties of enforced servitude.

It is with African slavery, perhaps the most gigantic scheme of traffic in human beings known to the annals of the race, that we are chiefly concerned—an institution that was inaugurated and fostered by the Christian nations of the modern world, and that perished at last through the force of a moral opposition to its continuance, which culminated in one of the most sanguinary conflicts of modern times.

African slavery in North America had its beginning in 1620, when a Dutch ship from the coast of Guinea visited Jamestown and sold a cargo of slaves to the planters of Virginia. From this small beginning commenced a traffic that brought untold wealth to the slave-dealers, and finally resulted in locating millions of the African race on American shores.

England must ever bear a large portion of the odium which mankind will ever attach to the wretched slave traffic, although it is but just to say that she was the first to lead in the fight for its abolition. For centuries, however, she kept this traffic alive by supplying the markets of her colonies and legalizing the traffic among her subjects. She chartered companies with exclusive rights to buy and sell slaves, and, in the reign of William and Mary, she no longer confined it to favored corporations, but authorized every subject of the crown likewise to engage in the inhuman business.

Bryan Edwards estimated that the total import of African slaves into all the British colonies of America and the West Indies between 1680 and 1786, to be 2,130,000, or an average of 20,095 per year for 106 years. It was not until the year 1833 that the English parliament, largely through the life-long efforts of William Wilberforce, passed what is known as the Emancipation bill, putting an end to slavery in the English domains. The bill abolishing the traffic in slaves was passed twenty-six years before, in 1807.

France, Spain, Portugal, Denmark and Holland must share with England the shame of the modern African slave-trade, and of fastening the institution of slavery upon America. In 1791 the number of European factories on the African coast for turning out slaves for the world was forty. Of these fourteen were English, three French, fifteen Dutch, four Portuguese and four Danish.

Thus it is seen that the hunting of human beings in Africa for the slave-markets of the world was legalized by the leading and most civilized

nations of the globe less than one hundred years
ago. All that power and wealth could do to bring
the traffic into existence, and to continue it for
over two hundred years, was done. The native
African chiefs were bribed by foreign money, and
thus induced to capture the wild savages of the
forests, sometimes making levies upon their own
immediate subjects to exchange them for com-
modities supplied by European slave trafficers
stationed along the coasts. We quote again from
the "Britannica" these words: "They often set
fire to a village by night and captured the inhabitants while trying to escape. Thus all that was
shocking in the barbarism of Africa was multiplied and intensified by this foreign stimulation."

"To the miseries thus produced, and to those
suffered by the captives in their removal to the
coast, were added the horrors of the middle passage. Exclusive of the slaves who died before
they sailed from Africa, twelve and one-half per
cent. were lost during their passage to the West
Indies, four and one-half per cent. while in har-
bors or before their sale, and one-third more in
the seasoning. Thus, of every lot of one hundred shipped from Africa, seventeen died in about
nine weeks, and not more than fifty lived to be
effective laborers in the islands. The circumstances of their subsequent life on the plantations
were not favorable to the increase of their num-

bers. In Jamaica there were, in 1690, forty thousand African slaves. From that year until 1820 there were imported 800,000, yet at the latter date there were only 340,000." The record does not show such great fatality with those cargoes shipped to what are now the United States, but it was a dark picture of suffering and cruelty.

I have thus briefly alluded to some general facts in the history of the introduction of African slavery into America, now happily abolished both as a traffic and an institution. It was born of the cupidity of mankind and kept alive for centuries for the ends of gain. That it was right, even those who once most heartily approved of and advocated it, would not now contend. It is, indeed, a painful page to look upon, and were it not, that through its dark lines we may now trace the mysterious guidings of Providence, it would be unrelieved by a single alleviating reflection.

The student of history, looking at it in the light of divine direction in the affairs of this world, may discover the purpose of God to accomplish his ends, overruling even the "wrath of man," and making it contribute to the consummation of his will.

The bondage of the Israelites in Egypt seemed a dark and inexplicable fate for the chosen children of God, but the outcome of it was the founding, forming and cementing of the Jewish nation, which was to play such an important part in all the subsequent history of the human race.

Who can tell, and the dawning light of the Divine purpose begins even now to reveal itself, but that it was to be, through this means, that the Almighty intends to work out the final redemption of the African race in these lands, and the far-off dark continent, which is now offering such fertile and inviting fields for missionary and evangelical effort and enterprise?

The Jewish nation, since its disintegration and scattering abroad, has passed through scarcely a less fiery baptism of suffering and cruelty than has fallen to the lot of the slave exiles from African shores. They have been hunted in all lands, despised, cast out and killed by the Gentiles, with whom they have been forced to dwell. It may be, too, that through their pathetic wanderings the golden thread of Providence runs, and that, redeemed and Christianized, they will some day return to their native land, and build up again the broken foundations of their once splendid kingdom which, in grandeur and glory, shall far surpass the greatness of the old Hebrew monarchy in its palmiest days, when the wealth and power of Solomon excited the admiration and wonder of the queen of Sheba.

At least while we may not approve, but even condemn the cruelty and inhumanity which led to

the introduction of African slavery upon this continent, and which marked and marred its continuance, we may yet believe that it was permitted by
the Almighty for wise and glorious purposes, and
will issue at length in the elevation of the negro
race to a condition of enlightened, Christian civilization he could not otherwise have attained.
How else can he interpret that Providence, which
permitted the existence of slavery so long, and
which, at length, as strangely and signally, put an
end to its existence, not only in the United States,
but in every country of the globe?

# CHAPTER III.

## THE EVILS OF AFRICAN SLAVERY.

IN considering this evil we are not to suppose that the negro was the only sufferer from it. The slave-holder was the victim of the indirect consequences of the system which was fraught with injury to all who were connected with it.

In what I am about to say I am free to admit that there were many humane masters—masters who were kind to their slaves, who afforded them every advantage and consideration possible under the system. But to preserve and perpetuate the system, it was necessary to keep the slave in ignorance and to ever remind him of his menial position. Laws were enacted prohibiting his learning to read or write, and his owner was authorized to inflict the most severe corporal punishment short of death. He could even delegate this authority to an agent, who, having no pecuniary interest in the slave, was often unspeakably cruel in the severity with which he exercised his delegated authority.

Such a system, practically placing no restraint upon the power and rights of the master, could but be abused and to what extent only the secrets of the final day will reveal.

Before pointing out the evils of slavery as it affected the slave himself, let us mention briefly its indirect consequences to the slave-holders.

First, it developed a class of landed gentry in the South, who, while they were not titled, were more absolutely lords than the dukes and earls and barons of England. The immense wealth, wrought for them by slave labor, exempted them from the necessity of toil, and removed all incentives to enter upon those bold enterprises requiring individual effort and push, which have given such distinctive strength and success to the citizenship of the North and West. For them, it was a day of luxurious ease, whiled away in amusement and pleasure, an era of idleness and sensuality, second only to that which marked the Augustan age of Rome when that empire reached the zenith of its wealth and glory, and which was the beginning and the cause of the final downfall of that colossal power. The splendid mansions of the Southern gentry, adorned with Doric columns, majestic and imposing, their rich and fertile fields stretching away in the distance white with the fleecy staple, their hundreds of slaves felling the forests and toiling on the old plantations, present a picture of lordly wealth and splendid ease, without a parallel in the history of the world. The

Roman patrician and the English lord were paupers beside this landed aristocracy of the South.

The consequence to these wealthy slave-holders was the dwarfing of the spirit of enterprise and genuine, robust manhood, of that strong self-assertive individuality which is the first requisite of a freeman. The Southern planter grew to be a pleasure lover, a dreamy epicurean, a worshipper at the shrine of ease and sensuality. His children grew up in the same atmosphere—strangers to toil and self-reliance. In tranquil languor they passed their lives, never having to strike one blow in the struggle for existence. For this condition slavery was responsible, and they reaped from it the harvest of a dwarfed physical development, and of a deadening industrial paralysis from which their descendants have not recovered to this day.

Even the poor whites, who owned no slaves, had to pay the penalty of their proximity to slavery. The slave-holder bought up as rapidly as he could the lands of the South, and the landless white denizen was elbowed off to the barren sections, or else forced to remain where the competition with slave labor was so sharp that he could scarcely find employment, or if he did, the wages he received were so scanty that he could barely subsist. In the race of life he had the smallest chance of success, and was doomed to live and die where the

conditions of his environment were well-nigh fatal
to his betterment.

Under the institution of slavery, the South was
limited in her industrial development to the single
line of agriculture. Slave labor was most. profit-
able in the cotton fields and on the sugar plantations. Here no skilled artisans, no trained me-
chanics were needed; only muscle and brawn were
required to till the soil, and gather its products.
As fast as wealth grew it was converted into more
slaves, and thus the industry and capital of the
South were confined to agriculture. But few factories were built. Manufacturing was at a discount. No great cities were founded and populated.
Commerce was neglected, shops, furnaces, mills,
and, indeed, every branch of industrial enterprise
was largely, if not wholly, neglected. These es-
tablishments were left to Northern money and
Northern enterprise. And, as history has not furnished a single instance of a people, devoted solely
to agricultural pursuits, rising to commanding and
permanent place and power, the logical inference
is that, under slavery, the South would have been
eventually the least prosperous section of the
Union, if the abolition of slavery had never been
effected. This fact made the South almost helpless at the close of the war between the States.
She will rise to industrial prosperity, now, only as
she diversifies her enterprises. This she is doing

rapidly, and this is one of the good results flowing from the abolition of slavery.

Time would fail us to enumerate the evils resulting to the moral character and social well-being of the Southern people from the presence of African slavery in their midst. The influence of this institution, in every moral view of it, was bad, and only bad. It developed a race of masters—a relation out of place in a world the Almighty intended to be free. Ownership in flesh and blood was never a right designed by God to be conferred on any man. It is fatal to him who exercises it, as well as to him upon whom it is exercised It creates a spirit of authority and of imperious haughtiness that destroys that brotherhood of men, which the Almighty made to be the relation of men.

The violence done to himself by the ownership of his human brother was one of the greatest evils the Southern slave-holders reaped from slavery. The involuntary servitude of the man whom God made as free himself, the groans and cries of human beings evoked by the lash in hands that wielded it only by the right of power, the appropriation of the products of toil not his own, the abasement and degradation of human souls for selfish aggrandizement—this was the spectacle the Southern slave-holder had daily to behold, and it was enough to blight his sense of moral responsibility, and destroy the God-given instinct of right as between man and man.

We might allude to the evil of miscegenation, an evil which began in slavery, and which is still going on with shameful flagrancy. It is not a matter of conjecture or supposition, but of history and fact, that the fairest and most comely negro girls were appropriated by the young white men of the South, and devoted to the ends of unholy lust; and to the family domestics thousands of mulatto children were born. This was bad enough, but, when to this was added the fact that these children were born slaves, and herded with slaves, and that these white fathers had to witness their own offspring growing up to lives of bondage, and subject to the whip of the overseer, it was enough to harden and blunt the sensibilities of their souls.

But why multiply arguments to show the evils of slavery upon the slave-holders themselves, when the white people of the South have long since seen and admitted them. Slavery, in its effects upon the white man, was scarcely less injurious than it was upon the slave himself.

The direct consequences of slavery upon the negro (none but God can estimate the ultimate outgrowth of it) were evil, and only evil.

First, in his case, as in the case of all slaves, it repressed all real manhood, and destroyed that individuality and aspiration of spirit, which are the first conditions of self-respecting character, either in an individual or in a race. Taught and compelled to obey, he could but walk in the marked-out path of another's will, and, hence, all independence and self-active power were denied him. He was simply a machine, a mere automaton, a tethered ox in a tread-mill, going the weary rounds of an appointed path, which he could not leave or change.

The thought of a life in which volition played a part was foreign to him, chained as he was to the will of a master. History furnishes no instance of individual or race elevation without the boon of personal liberty. Moral and intellectual advancement is as impossible to the slave as the sight of the sun is to the man without eyes. This was one of the most potent, as well as one of the most pathetic, evils incident to slavery, and the memory of it still brings tears to the eyes of those to whom the benighting influences of the system left sensibility sufficient to estimate the force of such deprivation.

The evils of slavery were augmented further by the ignorance it entailed. Enlightenment of the slave meant menace to the institution, and the Southern slaveholder was consistent when he enacted legislation forbidding the instruction of his slaves in the rudimentary branches of education. And so his lot was not only that of absolute servitude, but also of absolute ignorance. What argument could be made for an institution, the strongest pillar of which was ignorance? Is it possible that the Divine Being ever intended any of his creatures to live under conditions, the preservation of which demands the total and continual benightment of their minds and souls? The great mass of the negroes of the South grew up in dense ignorance, and the race to-day, though struggling up to some degree of knowledge, is suffering from the effects of that enforced ignorance.

It would be a work of unnecessary expense both of time and material, to enlarge upon the moral and religious injury the system of slavery inflicted upon the negro. In many instances, and we record it gratefully, religious instruction was afforded to the slave. Such men as Bishop Capers and Rev. William J. Sasnett, D.D., of the Southern Methodist Church, and Jesse Murcer and Dr. Mallory, of the Baptist Church, gave of their strength and money to preach and send the gospel to the benighted slaves of the South. But taking into the account all that was done by the pious ministers and laymen among the whites, the fact still remains that the multitudes of Southern negroes grew up, lived and died without adequate religious or moral instruction.

As a consequence, those moral principles and qualities which are the requisites of virtuous life, were dwarfed or wholly eradicated for the time. Many have harshly judged the colored race for the want of moral purity. They do not take into consideration their condition and environment for more than two hundred years. I believe it to be a fact, that no race, similarly situated, can show any better moral record than my own.

How could there be a moral atmosphere amidst the miasmatic surroundings of slavery? There could be no home in the true sense of that word, and hence no home instruction. There was no lawful wedlock. Husband and wife they were only in name, and these were separated at the caprice, cupidity or misfortune of their owner. Virtue was an impossibility when maternity in or out of wedlock was encouraged by the master and a premium put thereupon. The wonder is, that under such a system there could be found a single instance of moral purity among the whole race.

The physical evils of slavery were great. Punishment was meted out by the law of will, and stripes were the daily portion of the negro. No good can be accomplished by recalling the sufferings of that bondage time. Rather would we draw the veil of oblivion over it and forget it as we march on to the destiny of an enlightened, educated and useful citizenship.

I believe there are but a few among the whites of the South who would claim now that slavery was a blessing to either race. On the other hand the great masses of the Southern whites recognize what a tremendous injury it was to them as well as the slaves, and would not re-enact it if they could.

The time for its extinction had come in the order and by the will of Providence. That God will ultimately bring good out of this mighty evil, which pressed so long upon the South like a terrible incubus, I can but believe. When we as a race can stand upon the green fields of our appointed Caanan, emancipated not only from political bondage, but free from the shackles of vice and ignorance, we may be permitted to see that through all the dark way we came God was leading to final happiness and real freedom.

# CHAPTER IV.

## AGITATION BY ABOLITIONISTS.

WILLIAM WILBERFORCE, statesman, philanthropist and orator, is entitled to the first place among the great English leaders in the struggle for emancipation. In every place and on every occasion his eloquent voice was lifted against slavery. In parliament, on the hustings, on the rostrum he plead for the freedom of the negro. His pen, too, was enlisted in the cause he so much loved, until at length he literally created a moral sentiment in England which was resistless in its sweep and which ultimated at last in the complete triumph of abolition. Through his efforts, backed by many noble spirits, the Emancipation Bill, as has been already stated, was passed in August, 1833, one month after his death. He had given a lifetime to the work of lifting from his country the stigma of slavery, and died just as the accomplishment of his mission was in sight. Like Lincoln and John Brown, he was permitted to catch a view of the promised land, to the borders of which they had led the oppressed and down-trodden sons of Ham, but was not permitted to enter with them and behold their joy as they rested in the fertile fields and vine-clad hills of freedom. The name of William Wilberforce will live as long as liberty is prized and philanthropy is honored.

In America Wm. Lloyd Garrison stands at the head of the long list of agitators who finally triumphed against slavery. Many distinguished men, however, even before Garrison was born, are on record in American history as against the institution of slavery. George Washington was opposed to it, and in his last will inserted a clause providing for the manumission of his slaves. Thomas Jefferson, the author of the Declaration of Independence, recognized its evils, and no abolitionist ever used stronger language in condemning it. In speaking of the slaves he used the expression "our brethren," showing his recognition of the bond of a common humanity with the meanest slave that toiled in the tobacco fields of Virginia. But, notwithstanding the influence of these and other great names, slavery grew and spread in the South and Southwest, until at the beginning of the war between the states there were more than four millions of slaves in the United States.

To combat this growing evil Providence seemed to have raised up Wm. Lloyd Garrison, who was born at Newburyport, Mass., December 10th, 1805. His profound belief in his mission, his untiring devotion to it, his adaptation by nature for leadership in a great reform movement, his peculiar gifts as a writer, all conspired to make him an agitator and a leader of wonderful power.

It was in the *Genius,* a paper published in Baltimore, that he first began to espouse, publicly, the cause of immediate emancipation. His fiery denunciation of the system of slavery provoked at once the bitter resentment and opposition of the slaveholders of the South. A vessel, owned in Newburyport, transported a shipload of slaves from Baltimore to New Orleans. This procedure he characterized as an act of "domestic piracy," and declared his design to "cover with infamy" the participants in this shameful affair. He was prosecuted by the owner of the vessel, convicted, fined fifty dollars and costs of trial, and in default of payment thereof, was committed to jail. His conviction and imprisonment produced great excitement at the time throughout the whole country. The poet, John G. Whittier, interceded with Henry Clay, then a pro-slavery advocate, to pay the fine and secure the release of Garrison, but before Mr. Clay had time to comply, as he had consented to do, Mr. Arthur Tappan, a merchant of New York, discharged the fine and the costs, and Mr. Garrison was liberated after seven weeks of imprisonment.

Seeing the difficulty in prosecuting his crusade in an atmosphere so hostile, he at once dissolved his connection with the *Genius,* and established in Boston a paper, which he named the *Liberator.*

The first issue of this paper, which was destined to such a remarkable history, was published in January, 1831. In his editorial address to the people of the United States, he used these words, which have become memorable, "I am in earnest, I will not equivocate, I will not excuse, I will not retreat a single inch, and I will be heard." The paper began with little circulation and influence. Garrison was forced to sleep in the dingy apartments of his printing office, and it was with great difficulty that he kept the paper from suspending in the first few months of its existence. It lived on, however, growing in influence and circulation, until it became the mouthpiece of the Abolition party at the North. It lived to print President Lincoln's Emancipation Proclamation, and the Thirteenth and Fourteenth Amendments to the Constitution, forever prohibiting slavery in the United States of America.

The first society organized by Mr. Garrison was the New England Anti-Slavery Society, which issued its manifesto in 1832. In this same year Mr. Garrison published a work entitled, "Thoughts on African Colonization," in which he showed that the American Colonization Society was, in reality, an organization in the interest of slavery, and its principles and objects in no sense a remedy for the evils of slavery.

In 1833 Mr. Garrison went to England. There

he met Wilberforce, Clarkson, Buxton, O'Connell, George Thompson, and others, who gave him a cordial reception, and their hearty co-operation in his great work. He was successful in undeceiving the English people as to the design and character of the American Colonization Society, and brought back with him a protest against it, signed by Wilberforce, Thackeray, Macaulay, Gurney, Evans, Buxton, O'Connell, and many other distinguished anti-slavery gentlemen.

Mr. Garrison's visit to England enraged the pro-slavery people of the United States, and, upon his return, fresh outbursts of denunciation against him were heard on every hand, and mobs were organized to suppress the public discussion of the slavery question. Now was inaugurated what Harriet Martineau was pleased to call the "Martyr Age of America." The opposition to the Abolition movement was not confined to the South. It met violent resistance at the North, and Boston itself was the centre of mob violence against the Anti-Slavery agitators. Mr. Thomson, an English gentleman, and an eloquent Abolition speaker, who had come to America with Mr. Garrison, was treated with great indignity by the enemies of emancipation. His appearance in New England became the signal for a mob, and in 1835 he was compelled to return to England to save his life. Just before his departure it was announced that he would address the " Woman's Anti-Slavery Society of New England." This announcement brought out a mob of the society gentlemen of Boston, from whose violence, had he appeared at the appointed place, he would probably not have escaped with his life. The whole city was excited, and the mob seized Mr. Garrison, who, when they had well-nigh torn his clothing from him, was dragged through the streets of Boston by the wild and infuriated crowds, wrought up to fanatical fury. A rope was placed around his body, with which they evidently intended to hang him, had he not been rescued by the friends of law and order. He was placed in jail for security, and subsequently secretly carried out of the city by his friends.

For several years these outbreaks of violence were kept up here and there, but the flame of opposition to American slavery which had been kindled could not be extinguished, and waxed hot and hotter. In 1844 William Garrison was made president of the American Emancipation Society, which position he continued to hold until the day of emancipation, when it was disbanded. He labored with tongue and pen until he saw with joy the consummation of his life-work, and died in New York city May 24, 1879, in the seventy-fourth year of his age, and was buried in Boston, the scene of his trials and triumphs.

Time would fail me to record here the names

and work of all the great spirits who took part in the movement for the freedom of the African slaves in America. I will be pardoned for a brief allusion to some of the chief actors in that great and tragic drama, in the execution of which thousands perished on the battle-field or came forth to victory, at length wearing the laurels of enduring fame.

Wendell Phillips was the great orator of the anti-slavery crusade whose, eloquence pleaded the cause of freedom. As a speaker, with the exception of Henry Ward Beecher, he was above all others the popular favorite, and led on the crusade with a fiery and commanding eloquence. As Patrick Henry was the mouthpiece of the Colonies in their revolt from England, so Wendell Phillips was the voice of the American philanthropists who led on the movement to break the bondage of the negro in America and free him from his Southern master. Wendell Phillips has recently passed up to his reward, and millions of stars will gleam forever in his crown, standing for the millions of his race for whose liberty he plead, and perhaps did as much, as any instrument that Providence employed, to accomplish.

The negro in America can never forget the debt he owes to Mrs. Harriet Beecher Stowe for the services she rendered to the cause of his freedom. Her wonderful contribution to the literature of the

anti-slavery crusade in the volume entitled " Uncle
Tom's Cabin," did more perhaps to arouse universal sympathy for the American slaves and
crystallize sentiment for immediate emancipation
than any other one agency of Providence. And
yet at first it was coldly received, and the author
herself was sorely disappointed at the treatment
it was given, even by the anti-slavery public. She
says, speaking of the time when it was first issued : " It seemed to me that there was no hope ;
that nobody would hear, that nobody would read,
nobody would pity ; that this frightful system,
which had pursued its victims into the free
states, might at last threaten them even in
Canada."

Notwithstanding, in five years from the date of
the issue of this most wonderful book, nearly
500,000 copies were sold in the United States
alone. No book has ever had such a circulation
except the Bible, and no book ever accomplished
so much for the human race except the Bible. It
was read in the homes and by the firesides of the
North, and by the friends of freedom everywhere.
Its pathetic recital of the sufferings of the Southern negro drew tears from millions who had never
seen a slave, and created a hatred for the system
of slavery in countless human hearts. The good
woman whose " pen was as mighty as the sword,"
passed away a short while since, embalmed in the

love and grateful memory of those she helped to free.

Fred Douglas, whose mother was a negro slave in Maryland, must not be omitted from the record of those who took a conspicuous part in the annals of those times. He ran away from his home when quite a youth, and settled at New Bedford, Massachusetts. Here he changed his name from Loyd to Douglas. In 1841 he was offered the agency of the Massachusetts Anti-Slavery Society. In this capacity he traveled through the New England States for four years. Large audiences were attracted by his graphic descriptions of the evils of slavery, and by his eloquent appeals for sympathy and help on the behalf of his race. From this time on down to emancipation, he labored with his tongue and pen for the abolition of slavery in the United States. When the volume of the record is fully made up, it will be seen that this half-breed, Frederick Douglas, is not a whit behind the chiefest apostle of the gospel of liberty. He was honored by President Hayes as Recorder of Deeds and Marshal of the District of Columbia. President Harrison conferred upon him the post of Minister to Hayti. Thus this distinguished philanthropist and orator, perhaps the most deservedly famous man of his race in all its history, was honored by his country at last. He died in Washington city in February, 1895, and was buried with appropriate honors.

# CHAPTER V.

THE day of deliverance was now approaching. The crisis in the irrepressible conflict was near at hand. The South would listen to no compromise, and the Abolition party at the North was equally determined. God has decreed that there is to be no "let up" in the conflict between right and wrong, no cessation of hostilities between truth and error, no armistice in the battle between liberty and oppression. The struggle is on to the finish, and he is no part of a prophet that does not see in right, truth, and liberty, the conquering forces. Events may delay, but cannot finally defeat the triumph of these principles, anchored, as they are, to the throne of God. In the language of the poet:

> Truth crushed to earth will rise again,
> The eternal years of God are hers,
> But error wounded writhes in pain,
> And dies amid her worshippers.

From the bleak hills of the North and from the wide, flower-crowned plains of the West the bugle notes of freedom were sounded. The champions of liberty lifted aloud their clarion voices from the

41

forum, the hustings and in the Senate halls of the nation. " In thoughts that breathed and words that burned," the giants of freedom's cause uttered their anathemas against a system which had long been a blot on American civilization and a reproach to the Christian world. In song and oratory the sufferings and pains and wrongs of slavery were trumpeted forth to the world, that men might read and hear the pitiful story of the slave, and, impelled by the power of human sympathy, rally to the deliverance of the oppressed and down-trodden millions of the Southern negroes.

The first guns that were sounded were heard on the soil of Kansas. John Brown, born in Connecticut May 9th, 1800, was the revolutionary spirit that led the van of armed resistance against the growing pro-slavery spirit.

His four sons, residents of Ohio, moved to Kansas in 1854. They settled near the Missouri border in Lykins county. Partaking strongly of the anti-slavery views of their father, they were insulted, threatened and plundered by lawless bands of pro-slavery men from Missouri, and, at length, they invited their father to come to their aid, and to bring supplies of guns and ammunition. He was glad to obey the summons. For more than fifteen years he had been actively planning to overthrow and destroy the slave power, and now he deemed the set time had come to begin his

work, to strike the blow which would unify the
North and lead to a concerted, armed resistance
against the growing pro-slavery power.

Tough in sinew, athletic in build, of stern Puri-
tan ancestry, deeply religious in spirit, he was
singularly adapted to become a leader and a martyr
in the holy cause. In 1855, leaving his family
behind, he went to join his sons in Kansas, prepared to join battle with the pro-slavery forces,
and if it were God's will, to perish in the struggle.
In November of the same year the citizens of
Lawrence, the rallying point of the free-state men,
armed themselves to repel the attack of a large
body of Missourians, who, organized as Kansas
militia, had laid siege to the town. John Brown
received a command, took charge of his men and
counselled an immediate movement upon the Missourians. The leaders of the free-state men, un-
willing to bring on a collision, endeavored to adjust
matters by negotiation. This disgusted Brown,
who, in reply to an invitation from Gen. J. H.
Lane to attend a council of war, said : "Tell the
General when he wants me to fight to say so, but
that is the only order I will ever obey." Thence-
forth his operations were of an irregular character
and were conducted exclusively by himself. In
May, 1856, at the head of a small body of determined men, he went into camp on the Potta-
watomie, near the residence of his sons. A few

days later he was engaged in what was known as
the Black Jack fight, which resulted in the capture of a superior force of Missourians, with a considerable amount of goods which had been plundered on their marauding expedition.

In the latter part of August a fresh force of Missourians poured into Kansas, numbering nearly
two thousand men. A part of this force was
driven back by General Lane, while another body
of five hundred marched upon the town of Osa-
watomie, near which Brown was encamped with
about thirty men. In this encounter one of Brown's
sons was killed. Soon after this, Brown, seeing
that he could do little more in the West at that
time, left for the East.

In February, 1857, he addressed a committee of
the Massachusetts Legislature, and in Boston and
other cities he had frequent interviews with anti-
slavery sympathizers. His mission proved to be
an unsuccessful one, so far as securing substantial
help. The North was not yet ripe for the com-
mencement of the great conflict. Years of accumulating sentiment were yet necessary to precipitate the great national struggle, in which heroes
like John Brown were to press on in the agitation,
and die as martyrs to the cause.

With a small body of men John Brown repaired
to Iowa, where he passed the winter of 1857–58
in practicing military exercises. He now com-

manded his followers to go with him to Virginia, instead of Kansas, where, as they had supposed, he intended to commence his military operations. Omitting intermediate events, we find him beginning the Harper's Ferry campaign, in June, 1859 The "American Encyclopedia" furnishes the following account of that memorable historic chapter in the anti-slavery movement:

"In the latter part of June, 1859, John Brown appeared at Hagerstown, Md., where he represented himself to be a farmer, named Smith, from Western New York, in search of a cheap farm adapted to wool growing. He finally rented for a few months a farm in Virginia, about six miles from Harper's Ferry, which he occupied with several of his party early in July. Others joined him from time to time, including his three sons, until the force numbered twenty-two persons, of whom seventeen were white, and the remainder negroes. Boxes of arms, ammunition, and other supplies, which had been shipped to Chambersburg, Pa., were gradually removed to the farm in Virginia, without exciting the suspicion of the neighbors. In selecting this place for the first attack, he had for his purpose the capture of the United States Arsenal at Harper's Ferry, where were usually stored from one to two hundred thousand stands of arms. This building, with its contents, once in his possession, he expected to rally to his support the slave population of the neighborhood. When his forces were sufficiently recruited and equipped, he proposed to convey them into the free States, or, if that should prove impossible, to retire to the mountains, and inaugurate a general civil war.

"The night of October 24, 1859, was originally fixed for the attack upon the arsenal, but at a council called by Brown on Sunday, the 16th, it was determined to begin their operations that very evening. The presence of so large a body in the neighborhood, with no ostensible object, had begun to arouse the suspicions of the Virginians, and further delay was considered dangerous. About 10 o'clock on Sunday night, Brown and his men entered the village of Harper's Ferry, and, having extinguished the lights on the streets, took possession of the arsenal, overpowering and making prisoners of the watchmen, who formed the sole guard of the building. The watchman at the bridge across the Potomac was next captured, and the railroad train from the West, which arrived there shortly after 1 A.M., on the 17th, was stopped. During the night the houses of Colonel Washington and other citizens in the neighborhood were visited, and stripped of whatever arms they contained. The owners were imprisoned in the arsenal, and their slaves were freed. At daylight, on the 17th, the train was allowed to proceed toward Baltimore, Brown freely informing every one who questioned him that his object in seizing the arsenal was to free the slaves, and that he acted by the authority of God Almighty. As the morning advanced, he gathered in prisoners, principally from the male citizens, who appeared upon the streets, and the workmen, as they approached the arsenal to assume their daily avocations. By 8 o'clock the number exceeded sixty. Heywood, a negro porter at the railroad depot, was ordered by Brown's followers to join them. He refused, and, attempting to escape, was shot dead.

"The citizens by this time began to recover from the stupor into which the audacity of Brown's attack had plunged them. A desultory firing was opened upon the arsenal, and several persons were killed and wounded upon either side, including the mayor and one or two other prominent citizens and one of Brown's sons, but until noon Brown virtually held possession of the town. Up to that time his force had increased only by the accession of six or eight negroes, who were compelled by threats to join him.

"As the day advanced opposing forces gathered around him. The military from the neighborhood marched into the town, and the capturers of the arsenal soon found themselves closely besieged in the building. Of the two insurgents guarding the bridge, one was killed and the other was captured. Five men who occupied the rifle-works were driven out, and all were killed or captured. The arsenal was now surrounded on all sides by armed Virginians, who poured ceaseless volleys upon it, which were returned by Brown's men in the garrison. So greatly were the attacking forces incensed by the shooting of the mayor and other popular citizens, that when Aaron D. Stephens, one of Brown's most trusty followers, was sent out with a flag of truce, he was instantly shot down, receiving six balls in his body, and Thompson, the prisoner captured at the bridge, was put to death.

"By nightfall of the 17th the arsenal was completely invested by the military, and Brown retired with such of his prisoners as had not escaped to the engine-house, an attack upon which he repulsed with a loss of two killed and six wounded. Soon after this the firing ceased for the day. The situation was then desperate for Brown. His forces had dwindled down to three uninjured white men beside himself, and a few negroes from the neighborhood. The remainder were killed or mortally wounded with the exception of a half dozen who had been sent out in the morning to liberate slaves, and could not rejoin their chief. Brown nevertheless displayed, during the night, a coolness and self-control which extorted the admiration of his prisoners. "With one son dead by his side," says Col. Washington, "and another shot through, he felt the pulse of his dying son with one hand, held his rifle in the other, and commanded his men with the utmost composure, encouraging them to be firm, and to sell their lives as dearly as possible. He offered to release his prisoners provided his men were permitted to cross the bridge in safety." This offer having been rejected by the besiegers, the last avenue of escape was closed to him. During the night Col. Robert E. Lee, afterwards General Lee, of Confederate fame, with a body of United States marines and two pieces of artillery, arrived and took post near the engine-house.

"At seven o'clock on the morning of the 18th these troops battered in the door of the building, and in an instant overpowered the small garrison. Brown, fighting desperately to the last, was struck down by a sabre stroke, and while prostrate on the ground was twice bayonetted. Although grievously wounded, he preserved his undaunted bearing. When questioned as to his object in seizing the arsenal and imprisoning citizens, he answered with perfect frankness, but refused to compromise persons still at liberty. Governor Wise and Senator Mason, of Virginia, and Hon. C. L. Vallandigham, of Ohio, cross-examined him closely, but failed to elicit any other than a simple statement of his motives and personal acts. He declined to answer no reasonable question, asserting that he had only done his duty in attempting to liberate the slaves of Virginia, and that he had nothing to regret save the failure of the enterprise. He, however, expressed great solicitude for his son Watson, who was captured in a dying condition, and who died on Wednesday, the 19th. On the same day Brown and his surviving comrades were conveyed to the jail in Charlestown, Va. They were indicted a few days later for conspiring with negroes to produce insurrection, for treason against the commonwealth of Virginia, and for murder.

"On October 27th Brown was brought to trial. His request for a brief delay on the ground that he was mentally and physically unable to proceed with his trial, and that he wished to confer with counsel of his own choice instead of them assigned to him by the court, was denied. He was laid upon a cot within the bar, being too feeble to stand or even to sit, and in the presence of a court, violently prejudiced against him, conducted himself with singular calmness. He repelled with indignation the plea of insanity attempted to be urged in his behalf, and even offered, in order to save time and trouble, to identify papers in his own handwriting, which afforded strong evidence against him. Counsel meanwhile arrived from the North, and the trial went on. On the 31st he was found guilty on all the counts in the indictments, and on the succeeding day he was sentenced to be hanged on December 2nd.

" In the speech which he addressed to the court on this occasion, he disavowed any intention of committing murder or treason or the willful destruction of property. His 'prime object,' he said, ' was to liberate the slaves, not excite them to insurrection, and he therefore felt no consciousness of guilt.' He laid considerable stress upon his kind treatment of his prisoners in the arsenal, and he also expressed himself satisfied with the treatment he had himself received on the trial. During his imprisonment he received visits from his wife and a number of his Northern .friends, and held arguments on the slavery question with Southern clergymen who attempted to offer him the consolations of religion.

"On the day appointed for his execution he left the jail, an eye-witness said, with a radiant countenance and the step of a conqueror, pausing for a moment by the door to kiss a negro child, held up to him by its mother. On the scaffold he was calm, gentle and resigned, and warmly thanked all who had been kind to him during his imprisonment. Noticing that none but troops were present at the place of execution, he remarked that the citizens should not have been denied the privilege of coming to see him die. He met his death with perfect composure, and was apparently the least concerned of all present over the tragic events of the day."

Such is the brief account of the tragic part which this patriot and hero performed in the drama which is now forever historic. He, perhaps, did more than any other one man to crystallize sentiment and precipitate the conflict which at length resulted in the freedom of the negro. Some have classed him with zealots and fanatics, the victim of a mad enthusiasm. If this be so, Providence has indicated in a thousand ways His need of men of such order of mind and temperament. With a love of liberty which was unquenchable, and a courage which prompted him to follow his conviction to martyrdom itself, he was the one man of America to light the first torch of freedom which was at length to blaze into the light of liberty, in the beauty and splendor of which the darkness of slavery was to vanish forever. With the prejudices of the past left behind them, men of all sections are beginning to attribute to this long-despised man the high qualities of the philanthropist, the hero and the martyr, and to give him the bright place in history his sublime devotion to the right, as God gave him to see it, entitles him to fill. The colored people of the South should revere his memory and wreathe it with the laurels of honor and fame.

During the bloody war which soon followed his

death, millions marched to the music of his name, and wherever the legions of Grant, and Sherman, and Sheridan pressed on to victory might be heard the martial and inspiring strains of that now world-famed song,

> "John Brown's body lies mouldering in the ground,
> John Brown's body lies mouldering in the ground,
> As we go marching on."

# CHAPTER VI.

## LINCOLN AND OTHER LEADERS.

THE Abolition movement had many distinguished leaders. To Garrison, Wendell Phillips, Harriet Beecher Stowe, Fred. Douglas, and others must ever belong the honor of inaugurating it at a time when there were but few, even in the North, to favor it. At a later period in the agitation, however, many bold and powerful champions entered the lists, and did national and heroic service in the cause of freedom.

Among these, Abraham Lincoln was perhaps the most conspicuous. Not because he was the most ardent and enthusiastic, for there were thousands at the North who espoused the Abolition movement as heartily as did he, but because, by virtue of his official character and position, he was the representative leader in the struggle.

Lincoln was a Kentuckian by birth, but emigrated to Illinois in 1830, when he was twenty-one years of age. It was a strange, yet significant, circumstance that the great Moses of the new exodus should have been born and reared in a slaveholding State. It took a man strong enough to rise above the prejudice of birth and his earlier environments to head a movement which demanded, for its successful accomplishment, the sternest and most heroic qualities of soul.

His early advantages were meagre indeed, having never received but one year's schooling. Inured to a life of toil and poverty, he knew from actual experience the sufferings and trials of the poor. To this experience, perhaps more than to all else, may be attributed those warm and tender sympathies, which so marked and beautified his character, and made him the friend of the down-trodden and oppressed.

On a trip to New Orleans in a flat-boat in 1831, he saw for the first time slaves chained and scourged, and from that moment dates his life-long detestation of slavery. In 1837, when he was a member of the Legislature in Illinois, the Democratic majority passed some pro-slavery resolutions, against which he, and a member named Stone, entered a protest on the journal of the House. Thus, in the very outset of his political career, he recorded his opposition to slavery, and allied himself with the movement, of which, in subsequent years, he was to become the loved and immortal leader. Eleven years later, in 1848, while a member of the Lower House of Congress, he voted for the reception of anti-slavery petitions, inquiring into the constitutionality of slavery in the District of Columbia. On January 16, 1849, he introduced a bill abolishing slavery in the District, and compensating the slave-holders, provided the majority of the citizens should vote for it. In his speeches in the memorable contest with Stephen A. Douglas, his competitor for the United States Senate in 1858, he always stood for the prohibition of slavery in all the territories of the United States.

He was elected President of the United States in November, 1860, and on March 4, 1861, he entered upon the duties of that high and honorable position. It is due to the truth of history to say that Mr. Lincoln did not, in the outset of his official career as the great head and leader of the Republican party at the North, contemplate the unconditional emancipation of the Southern slaves. The South knowing that his election to the Presidency meant at least the prohibition of slavery in the territories, for Mr. Lincoln by every token had committed himself against its extension beyond its then recognized bounds, seceded at once from the union of states, and set up an independent government of its own, styled the "Confederate States." It was to preserve the Union that the North appealed to arms. Could this have been done without the abolition of slavery, doubtless slavery would have yet been in existence in the Southern States, or, at least, gradual emancipation, including compensation to slaveholders, would have been the tardy solution of the slavery question. But Providence had a hand in the revolution and events, over which human agencies had no control, rapidly hurried on the hour when the fate of the Union cause itself involved the emancipation of the negro.

On January 1, 1863, nearly two years after his inauguration, Mr. Lincoln issued his celebrated Emancipation Proclamation. It was as follows:

" Now, therefore, I, Abraham Lincoln, President of the United States, by virtue of the power in me vested as commander-in-chief of the army and navy of the United States, in time of actual armed rebellion against the authority and government of the United States, and as a fit and necessary war measure for repressing said rebellion, do on this first day of January, 1863, and in accordance with my purpose so to do publicly proclaimed for the full period of one hundred days from the day of the above first-mentioned order (alluding to his *pronunciamento* of September 1, 1862, in which he declared his purpose of issuing an emancipation proclamation unless the South laid down her arms and returned to the Union), and designates as the states and parts of states the following, to wit: Arkansas, Texas, Louisiana, except the parishes of St. Bernard and Plaquimine, Jefferson, St. Charles, St. John, St. James, Ascension, Assumption, Terra Bonne, La Fourche, St. Mary, St. Martin and Orleans, including the city of New Orleans, Mississippi, Alabama, Florida, Georgia, South Carolina, North Carolina, Virginia, except the forty-eight counties designated as West Virginia, and also the counties of Berkeley, Accomac, Northampton, Elizabeth City, York, Princess Anne and Norfolk, including the cities of Norfolk and Portsmouth, and which excepted parts are for the present left precisely as if this proclamation were not issued, and by virtue of the power and for the purpose aforesaid, I do order and declare that all persons held as slaves within such designated states, on and henceforward shall be free, and that the executive government of the United States, including the military and the naval authorities thereof, will recognize and maintain the freedom of said persons. And I hereby enjoin upon the people so declared to be free, to abstain from all violence, unless in necessary self-defence, and I recommend to them in all cases, when allowed, they labor faithfully for reasonable wages; and I further declare and make known that such persons of suitable condition will be received into the armed service of the United States to garrison forts, positions, stations and other places, and to man vessels of all sorts in said service. And upon this, sincerely believed to be an act of justice warranted by the Constitution upon military necessity, I invoke the considerate judgment of mankind and the gracious favor of Almighty God.

" In witness whereof I have hereto set my hand and caused the seal of the United States to be affixed."

The assassination of Lincoln in the closing hours of the war, when the battle to which his wisdom and patriotism had contributed so much, was just ending in triumph, was a tragedy full of the deepest pathos. Like Wolfe, on the field of Quebec, and Gustavus Adolphus, on the plains of Lutzen, he died in the moment of victory, and wore upon his cold, dead brow the wreath of a conqueror. His untimely death was a sad blow to the colored people of the South. His wisdom and influence in the shaping of affairs would, doubtless, have mitigated to some extent the evils of reconstruction days. The colored people would have followed his leadership with confident assurance and even the white people of the South would have regarded his counsels as they would those of no other Northern leader. Like Moses of old, however, he was not permitted to enter in and possess the Canaan to which he had led the suffering and defenseless thousands longing for freedom. From Nebo's summit of victory, however, he saw the beautiful fields of liberty, and died with his eyes fixed on the flower-crowned hills which stretched beyond. The tramp of the millions crossing the Jordan, whose waves his magic wand had parted, made music for his dying spirit, and he passed up through the clouds into the heavens with their songs of deliverance falling so sweetly upon his ears that he could scarcely distinguish the farewell music of earth from the welcoming music of heaven.

Abraham Lincoln will live in history as long as America is a republic. With Washington, Jefferson and Grant, he will go down to immortal fame. The colored people of America have enshrined his memory in their hearts, and there he will abide more secure than in the storied hatchments of marble or the towering shafts of brass or bronze.

Henry Ward Beecher, the prince of American pulpit orators, was almost as conspicuous in the pulpit and on the platform in the battle against slavery as Lincoln was in the forum and the cabinet. With a splendid presence, a voice of marvellous magic and compass, and an eloquence which moved the hearts of men as if it had been the voice of God speaking to them, he stood up as the great moral leader of the revolution. In England as well as America, he voiced the ever-growing sentiment of freedom, and in this country and on foreign shores he rallied the dallying millions to the solid attitude of decision.

No great movement was ever carried to final and permanent triumph that did not have back of it a great moral principle. It was here that Henry Ward Beecher realized that the appeal was to be made, and the final victory achieved. Beecher spoke to the conscience of America and the civilized world. Political orators addressed mainly the intellect, and discussed the question of slavery in the cold light of abstract human rights. They denounced it for political or sectional reasons, appealing often to the low motives of sectional jealousy and state rivalry. Beecher left behind him all economic or sectional questions, and appealed directly to the religious sentiment of the country and the world. Perhaps no speech ever made such a deep and powerful impression in this country as the one in which he sold from the block a beautiful and innocent girl, in scenic imitation of this legalized custom at the South.

But time would fail me to mention all the illustrious names which illumine and glorify the annals of those times, of Sumner, the chaste and courtly gentleman and scholar; of Greeley, the ready and eloquent writer; of Thaddeus Stevens, the courageous and aggressive commoner; of William Seward, the wise and prudent statesman, and others who gave their lives, their labors, their fortunes to this cause. They are embalmed in the grateful memory of the negro, and will live in history as long as philanthropy is honored, and unselfish devotion to liberty is admired.

# CHAPTER VII.

## THE CIVIL WAR AND THE PART THE NEGRO TOOK IN IT.

MANY people are ignorant of the part the negro took in the late Civil War in which his own freedom was the issue at stake. The records, so far as we can secure them, will be given in this chapter. They show that he was not altogether a passive looker-on, but that he did take an active part whenever and wherever he was free to do so.

Many reasons can be assigned to show why he could not as a race join the armies that were battling for his freedom and demonstrate that his conduct during that memorable conflict was not only commendable, but in the highest degree heroic.

If any are disposed to charge him with cowardice, let them consider first his helplessness. He was both ignorant and poor. He had no arms or munitions of war. The scene of the actual combat was as a rule distant from those sections in which the negro population was most dense. Many of the most populous sections were never reached by the Union armies, and even in those sections reached, the Federal authorities advised them against leaving their helpless wives and children, who had to be maintained by their labor.

The Southern slaves were very ignorant. They knew nothing of the use of arms or the art of war. They were as children when it came to battle in the science of modern warfare. How helpless are that people who know nothing, not only of the elements of knowledge, but have no acquaintance even with the geography of the country in which they live?

The negro is by nature docile and kind-spirited. Active participation on the part of the negroes, as a whole people, meant internecine strife, meant insurrection, meant untold suffering to helpless women and children. Such conduct would not only not have been heroic, but would have been barbarous and cruel. It would have been equivalent to the desertion of their wives and children, and to plunging the country into a scene of massacre and butchery that would have shamed the bloody cruelties of the French revolution.

Again, even if he had been sufficiently enlightened, and there had been no domestic reasons for his keeping aloof from the conflict, the scattered condition of the negro would have rendered it impossible for him to have engaged in it as a race. The slave population extended from Maryland to Texas. Guarded and watched with sleepless vigilance, there was no opportunity for concerted action. Any effort at co-operation could have been easily thwarted. It was simply impossible to bring such a large number of people together under the circumstances of their situation.

It is not a matter of surprise, then, when we consider these things, that the negro, as a race, made no concerted effort to assist in securing his own freedom. It would have been the most disastrous step he could have taken.

Not only so, but it will be to his everlasting credit that he did not—that he stood still and waited for the " salvation of God." While the flower and chivalry of the South were away from their homes, their families were treated with kindness and even tenderness, and no acts of violence can be charged to the negroes during that terrible time. There was no incendiarism, no murdering of the innocent, no deflouring of the virtuous, no pillage and plundering. I know of no crimes of rape or arson or massacre charged to the colored people during the four years of that bloody Civil War. The negro had no disposition to commit crimes like these, and this same disposition prompted him, as a race, to be quiet while God and his friends fought his battles for him. The Southern white man who can charge the negro with cowardice because he chose not to rise up as a whole race under all the circumstances of his condition and kill and slay, is heartless and ungrateful. History presents no sublimer spectacle than the patience and non-resistance of this race who, though smarting under the wrongs of more than two hundred years, refused to take revenge into their own hands and rebel with violence and bloodshed against their oppressors. No race ever acted more like Jesus Christ, whose life was one long, patient non-resistance to wrong.

While all this is true, yet it is fair to the colored race that they should have due credit for the honorable part they took in the Civil War. It is not generally known, though the record is open to the inspection of all, that the negro did take an active and honorable part in the war for his freedom. "Appleton's American Encyclopedia," page 494, contains the following:

"Colored soldiers were first enlisted into the Federal service in January, 1863, and within the year their number reached 100,000—about 50,000 actually bearing arms. Before the close of the war, they numbered about 170,000. These were not assigned as State troops, though credited to the quotas of the States from which they enlisted, but mustered in as United States Colored Volunteers."

Lieutenant Chas. A. Totten, of the United States Army, quotes from the Surgeon-General of the United States Army in 1870, to show that there were killed in battle, and died by disease or from wounds, 33,380 colored troops during the war between the States. This record speaks volumes for the courage and fidelity of the colored troops.

This is, indeed, a creditable showing, and demonstrates that the negro was not averse to fighting for his own freedom, when the opportunity was given him to honorably do so. He was not willing to butcher and slay, to be guilty of murder, rapine and arson, even to secure his own freedom; but he was willing to go forth as a soldier, and fight in honorable, open warfare. And this he did when he had the opportunity. As a soldier, the record shows that he was brave and chivalrous, and that he went gallantly into the thickest of the battle when duty called.

That the colored man not only makes a good citizen when properly educated, but that he makes a good soldier, is further shown by the fact that the United States has in its service at the present time the following efficient and well-trained colored troops:

| COLORED REGIMENTS. | ARM OF THE SERVICE. |
| --- | --- |
| Ninth. | Cavalry. |
| Tenth. | Cavalry. |
| Twenty-fourth. | Infantry. |
| Twenty-fifth. | Infantry. |

Three colored men have graduated from the West Point Military Academy, and there is one colored officer in the United States Army, Charles

Young, first lieutenant. There are three colored chaplains at present in the United States Army, viz.: Allen Allensworth, chaplain of the Twenty-fourth Infantry; Geo. W. Prioleau, chaplain of the Ninth U. S. Cavalry, and Theophilus G. Stewart, chaplain Twenty-fifth U. S. Infantry. Each of these chaplains have the rank of captain.

Thus it will be seen that the negro is coming to the front as a soldier, as well as a citizen.

It must not be thought that the colored people, who were not enlisted in the service during the late war, were passive and uninterested spectators of that mighty struggle waged for their freedom. They would have been less than human had they not been profoundly interested. Their prayers ascended for their deliverance, and their hearts yearned for the success of their friends. They fondly hoped for the hour of victory, when the night of slavery would end, and the day-dawn of freedom appear. They often talked to each other of the progress of the war, and conferred in secret as to what they might do to aid in the struggle, but they always decided it was the will of Providence that they should stand still, and see the salvation of God.

That they were right in their attitude, subsequent events have abundantly proved. God had determined to deliver them in a way which would exclude all boasting and self-gratulation. The negro was to achieve his freedom, not by his own exertion and strength, but by the power of the Lord God Almighty. Just as the Israelites were liberated by the special interposition of Providence, so was the negro. And that negro is indeed blind to the facts of history and ungrateful to the God of battles, who does not recognize the hand of Jehovah in his emancipation.

I think it due to the people of the North to say that there was little effort on their part to stir the passion of hatred and bloodshed in the heart of the negro during the war. While they encouraged every legitimate and honorable effort of the colored people to forward the cause of their freedom, they did not counsel riot and insurrection, and I believe it is true, that during the four years of that bloody conflict, there was not a single thoroughly-organized and executed insurrectionary uprising.

Many liberal-hearted Southerners have spoken eulogies upon the conduct of the negroes during that time. They have recognized the fact of their splendid behavior to their defenceless wives and children, and given this sentiment voice in poetry as well as prose. It should not be forgotten by the white people of the South, and they should ever remember with grateful affection the people who bore so patiently their wrongs, and waited so unresistingly the result of that memorable struggle. They should raise their voices now in protest in return for the kindness shown their wives and children in that perilous time, against the heartless mobs that often take up innocent negroes upon mere suspicion or for some fancied insult, and hang them from the nearest tree.

The negroes, as a race, not only took no part in any insurrectionary uprising during the war, but they quietly worked along in the fields, raising food supplies for the people. Left almost alone on the plantations, they protected the wives and children of their enslavers, and saw that they were done no violence. Though the wrongs of two hundred years were fresh in their memories, they had no heart to avenge them. They felt kindly to their owners in most instances, and were willing to leave the issue in the hands of heaven. They cared not to purchase their freedom by deeds of cruelty and wicked violence.

When in after years the full history of that great struggle shall be written in the calm and dispassionate light of truth and time, it will be the judgment of mankind that no grander spectacle is presented in human history than the attitude of the colored race during that stormy period. With a patience that never wearied, and a faith that never faltered, they awaited the will of heaven. Worn with long bondage, yearning for the boon of freedom, longing for the sun of liberty to rise, they kept their peace and left the result to God.

Here is a field for the epic poet, a theme for the lyrist and the psalmist. No stain of blood is on the fair escutcheon of the Southern slave. No chapter, crimsoned with blood and violence, tells the history of that terrible time. No property was burned, no maidens defloured, no murders committed. Neither the hope of liberty, nor the successes of the Northern army, could tempt the negro to rapine, arson, or murder. God be thanked that we can point to such a record, and that we can boast such a history. As we march on to triumph over ignorance, prejudice, oppression, and sin, we can ever carry in our bosoms the consciousness of having been merciful to those who were our captors, and, above all, of having done our duty as God gave us to see it.

Let our brothers in white remember these things in our favor, and, when tempted to be cruel and harsh with us, listen to the whisperings of gratitude, and extend to us that mercy and love we showed to them. Oh! ye Southern whites! among whom we live, and with whom in the same soil we expect to lie at last, let your hand of love go out to your poor, struggling brother in black, who has toiled so long through the weary night of ignorance and servitude, and help to lift him to the same heights of knowledge and virtue upon which you so proudly stand.

# CHAPTER VIII.

### THE RISE TO FREEDOM.

THE first breath of liberty to the colored man was like the intoxicating odors of Eden to our first parents. For two hundred years he had known nothing but toil and the self-abasement of the slave. In the cotton fields, and on the rice plantations of the South, he had worn his life away. In vain he looked through the sorrows of the night for joy to come in the morning. Stripes and the stocks were familiar to him, for even under the most humane master he was still subject to the lash.

But now the dawn of a new day had come, and the light of liberty was more welcome to him than the sunrise to the weary pilgrim of the night. As it broke over the hill-tops of the South, its splendid beams well-nigh dazzled his eyes, and he could scarcely believe that the night was gone, and the glorious day of freedom was at hand.

I shall never forget the moment when I heard the first tidings proclaiming liberty to the captive. Memory holds that hour as the most beautiful and enrapturing in all the history of a life which has alternated between the experience of a debasing

71

servitude and that of a joyous and unfettered freedom.

I was ploughing in the fields of Southern Georgia. The whole universe seemed to be exulting in the unrestraint of the liberty wherewith God has made all things free, save my bound and fettered soul, which dared not claim its birthright and kinship with God's wide world of freedom. The azure of a Southern sky bent over me and the air was fragrant with the fresh balm-breathing odors of spring. The fields and the forests were vocal with the blithe songs of birds, and the noise of limpid streams made music as they leaped along to the sea.

Suddenly the news was announced that the war had ended and that slavery was dead. The last battle had been fought, and the tragedy that closed at Appomattox had left the tyrant who had reigned for centuries slain upon the gory field.

In a moment the pent-up tears flooded my cheek and the psalm of thanksgiving arose to my lips. "I am free," I cried, hardly knowing in the first moments of liberty what and how great was the boon I had received. Others, my companions, toiling by my side, caught up the glad refrain, and shouts and rejoicings rang through the fields and forests like the song of Miriam from the lips of the liberated children of Israel.

Oh! the rapture of that hour! the bewildering

joy of that happy day! I would not say one
word to wound my white brethren in the South,
with whom I live and among whom I expect to
die, but to my dying day I can never forget the
delight of that, the first draught of freedom.

I felt the chains fall from my limbs, the gloom
lift from my soul, the manacles drop from my
hands. I heard the bolts break and saw the
prison door fly open. I caught the hands of the
angel and walked forth to the beautiful light. I
gazed upon the hills of freedom and breathed the
health-giving air. I snatched up the flowers
blooming at my feet, pressed them to my heart
and then kissed their scented lips in return for
their welcoming smiles. I ran, I leaped for joy.
I saw the smile of God. I heard the anthems of
the angels. A new world was at hand, and I
walked it, I imagine, with something of the rapture with which the angels walk the streets of
gold. Oh! never till I enter the gates of the city
of the New Jerusalem and wander along by the
river of life, purling through the gardens of God,
can I be happier than in that first hour of freedom.

I realized that all that life meant was mine at
last. Before it had been one long nightmare, one
dark journey of weariness and woe. From my
prison bars I had caught glimpses of the world of
liberty without, but now I could see it, bathe my
spirit in its sunshine and bask in its unobstructed

and unclouded splendor.  Surely it was enough to inspire and transport the heart, and make it beside itself with the very delirium of joy.

This picture is not overdrawn.  Thousands whose minds had not been wholly benighted by the repressing influences of slavery, and whose natures still possessed the capability of responding to the blessed boon of freedom felt as I did.  I have often thought of the joy that thrilled the Greeks when the victory at Marathon had delivered them from the Persian power, which meant their enslavement and ruin, and later, of their triumph at Salamis, when, for the second time, the same power strove to subdue them and blot Greek civilization from the world.  I have often pictured in imagination the joy of the inhabitants of France, when Joan of Arc, mounted on a snow-white charger, routed the veteran columns of England and led the trembling king to his coronation.  But the rejoicings of these delivered people were not greater than the exulting happiness of the four millions of Southern slaves in the first days and months of their newly-acquired freedom.

But as men get accustomed even to happiness, and lose the intense delight of joy itself when they get used to such an experience, it was not long before the freedmen began to find out that even freedom was not an unconditional blessing. They discovered that they needed more than mere political liberty, and, in the presence of the mighty problems that confronted them, they grew serious and thoughtful.

They were poor—very poor. Freedom they had, and nothing more—nothing but muscle and sinew, and faith in God. Four millions of people faced the struggle for existence without a dollar. No such spectacle has been witnessed in the world since the children of Israel crossed the Red Sea, and began their wanderings in the wilderness. No lands, no houses, no cattle, no sheep, no household goods, not even clothes and shoes. The spectacle was indeed appalling, but not without the glintings of hope. Labor was needed for Southern plantations, and *that* this hardy race could supply. The charge of thriftlessness and indolence has little to support it when we remember the absolute poverty of the negro on the day of his emancipation, and the immense wealth his labor has created for the South and himself since that day. Mostly by his free labor the cotton production of the South has grown from 3,000,000 to 9,000,000 bales. All other products of agriculture in the Southern States have increased in like ratio. The United States government has contributed but little to his physical wants, and, practically unaided, he has had to rely upon his own brawny arm for the means of subsistence. This was no small matter, and to meet all the demands upon him, he has had to give to it the best thought of his brain and the best work of his hands.

Another subject presented itself to the negro mind, after the first joys of freedom had expended themselves. It was the question of his education. No race ever came suddenly into the acquisition of freedom so thoroughly ignorant. It was the design of slavery to keep the slave in ignorance. The perpetuity of the system demanded it. Hence, when he was freed he could neither read nor write. He knew nothing of how to get along in the world of trade, and had no knowledge of the ordinary occupations and vocations of life. He was an easy prey to the designing and conscienceless employer, if he wished to rob him of the products of his labor. He knew but little of the amenities of life, having been accustomed to nothing but the primitive society common to the backwoods and remote sections of the South, and having been always treated as a menial, and not as a freeman and a citizen. He knew but little of law and government, and was easily duped by the designing politician, who used him wherever he could to further his own petty and ignoble ambitions. What a burden for a people to carry? How it hinders in the race for progress! As to what the negro has accomplished within the last thirty years towards removing this burden from his race, we will attempt to show in another chapter.

Another embarrassing question presented itself
to the negro upon his emancipation, and that was
his peculiar relation to the whites. His former
relation was at an end. His new relation was full
of perplexing and dangerous problems, some of
which are unsolved to this hour. On the one side
there was disdain and proud contempt, on the
other there was suspicion and distrust. I do not
allude to these things in the spirit of criticism and
complaint now. Perhaps this state of things was
natural and inevitable. History has no parallel
to the situation of the two races in the South immediately after the war. Four millions of slaves,
representing millions and billions of dollars, had
been freed, after one of the bloodiest wars that
history records. Stripped of all side-issues, this
had been the *casus belli*, and the war was fought
through on the question of slavery. The South
had just lost, and her people were exhausted and
impoverished. For this result the negro had to
bear the brunt of the South's discontent and disappointment. Her people could ill-brook the
slightest evidence of self-assertion and independence of spirit on the part of the colored people.
They must still wear the aspect and demean themselves after the manner of slaves. They must
never meet the white man on terms of equality,
but must yield to him the most abject homage and
deference. This, too, I am free to admit was but

a natural result of the passing away of the institution of slavery.

Nevertheless it was a serious menace to the peace and safety of the negro. Collisions arose, lawless bands and midnight marauders were organized, and the Ku Klux Clan became a terror to the defenceless negroes, who dreaded their approach under the cover of night, as did the Saxons of old the incursions of the Danes. In many instances, their humble homes were invaded by these lawless bands, and colored men were shot to death, or, if their lives were spared, they were cruelly beaten. It is not pleasant to recall these bloody and cruel scenes, and I am just enough to say that such outrages never received the sanction of the best class of Southern whites. I allude to these things to show the peculiar situation of the colored people of the South immediately after the advent of freedom, and in what embarrassing circumstances they were placed to work out their destiny.

This condition of things forced upon his attention the consideration of another question, and that was the one of habitation. Must he remain and suffer these indignities and cruelties, or must he leave and find some country where these race troubles would not perplex and annoy him so? Many and various schemes were presented to him. At first the negro took kindly to them all, and great excitement was aroused on the question of removal to distant states and countries. Many ship-loads left for Africa, and hundreds braved the dangers of a bitter climate and turned their faces toward the North and West. These schemes of emigration were at length found to be, for the most part, impracticable and ill-advised. After many unsuccessful attempts to leave his Southern *habitat*, and after the expenditure of a vast amount of unnecessary talk and enthusiasm, the negro, as a race, reached the conclusion to remain where he was. That he acted wisely in this decision, I will attempt to show in another chapter.

Finally, in this connection, the thoughtful and observing negroes soon discovered that the moral condition of their race was lamentably inadequate to meet the requirements of their new responsibilities. Under the repressing influences of slavery it was impossible to educate the negro to a high sense of religious and moral obligation. No people are prepared for freedom who are not enlightened as to the great principles of morality and religion. Nations fall for lack of these perpetuating and vitalizing forces. They rise in power and glory in the same scale as they rise in virtue, morality and Christianity. The joy of freedom was discounted in the minds of those who were intelligent enough to know the meaning of such a lack, when they beheld the moral status of their race. Here was a serious problem. To have self-respect, to have the consideration of the world, they knew that their people must be taught to regard virtue, honesty and integrity of character. Their wives, and sisters, and daughters, must have instilled into their minds and hearts the refining influences of Christian principles, so that they would rightly estimate the value of purity of life and character.

To this work the better class of the race addressed themselves. From the pulpit and the school-house the beauty of modesty and the sanctity of the marriage relation were insisted upon. That there has been improvement none will deny, as flagrant as is this vice of social impurity still. Yet in those families and communities where there has been protection afforded and religious truth inculcated, the colored women of the South are as pure as any in the world. In the absence of this instruction and protection, the opposite is true, not only among the colored people, but among all people.

These were some of the problems that made the wise negro tremble with apprehension after the first delight and joy of freedom had been experienced. No race was ever so suddenly thrown amid such difficult and perplexing circumstances. Nothing but the divine leading could have helped them even to a partial solution of the puzzling questions.

Thirty-two years of freedom tells a story of progress and improvement, I believe, unparalleled in the history of the world.  I know that the distance between my race and an ideal civilization is still almost infinite.  I know, too, that we have had the advantage of contact with Anglo-Saxon civilization.  Still I believe that the advance the colored people of the South have made, counting both the advantages and disadvantages of the case, since they were free, is the most marked and rapid in the annals of the human race.

# CHAPTER IX.

## THE RISE TO CITIZENSHIP.

THE slave was not a citizen. He could claim under the law no right but the right to live. He was in the category of goods and chattels. Under the evils incident to his condition it was almost impossible to secure him even in the right of life. Many masters were humane and their pecuniary interest in the slave prompted them to protect, as far as they could, the life of the slave, but even with the promptings of humanity and the motives of self-interest, the humane master could not always see to the protection of the lives of his slaves. Irresponsible and cruel overseers, far from the eye of the owner, sometimes exercised the most brutal treatment toward the defenseless negroes far away on the plantations. How many lost their lives sooner or later as the result of such treatment the records of the last day will alone disclose.

But now the dark night, so full of suffering and unrequited toil, was gone forever. The blood of thousands shed on the battle fields, which are now historic, had bought the negro's freedom. As much as the Southern whites resisted his further advancement, it was impossible to resist the tide of sentiment at the North, which now demanded that the negro be clothed with the full rights and immunities of citizenship. The Thirteenth Amendment to the Constitution passed Congress and was ratified by two-thirds of the States of the Union in 1865. This amendment simply abolished slavery in the United States. It was couched in the following language:

" Neither slavery nor involuntary servitude, except as a punishment for crime whereof the party shall have been duly convicted, shall exist within the United States or any place subject to their jurisdiction."

Three years later the Fourteenth Amendment was passed by Congress, and was ratified by the States. Many of the prominent men of the South, as we have already stated, advised acceptance of the situation and quiet submission to the results of the war. These far-sighted men saw that it was useless to fight the inevitable. For this they were socially ostracised, and even execrated by the white masses of the South. Hon. Benjamin H. Hill, to whom I have already alluded as the leading orator of the South, advocated the social ostracism of white Republicans, and in his celebrated " Notes on the Situation," hurled red-hot anathemas upon the heads of all who dared to advocate submission to reconstruction.

Notwithstanding, however, the Fourteenth Amendment became the law of this country in 1868. We give its text:

"All persons born or naturalized in the United States and subject to the jurisdiction thereof, are citizens of the United States, and of the State wherein they reside. No State shall make or enforce any law which shall abridge the privileges or immunities of citizens of the United States; nor shall any State deprive any person of life, liberty or property without due process of law, nor deny to any person within its jurisdiction the equal protection of the law. Representatives shall be apportioned among the several States according to their respective numbers, counting the whole number of persons in each state, excluding Indians not taxed, but when the right to vote at any election for the choice of electors for President and Vice-President of the United States, representatives in Congress, the executive and judicial officers of a State, or the members of the Legislature thereof, is denied to any of the male inhabitants of such State being twenty-one years of age and citizens of the United States are, in any way abridged, except for participation in rebellion or other crimes, the basis of representation therein shall be reduced in the proportion which the number of such male citizens shall bear to the whole number of male citizens in such State. No person shall be a senator or representative in Congress or elector for President and Vice-President, or hold any office civil or military under the United States or under any State who, having previously taken an oath as a member of Congress or as an officer of the United States, shall have engaged in insurrection or rebellion against the same, or given aid or comfort to the enemies thereof. But Congress may by a vote of two-thirds of each house remove such disability. The validity of the public debt of the United States authorized by law, including debts incurred for payment of pensions and bounties for services in suppressing insurrection or rebellion, shall not be questioned. But neither the United States nor any State shall assume or pay any debt or obligation incurred in aid of insurrection or rebellion against the United States, or any claim for the loss or the emancipation of any slave; but all such debts, obligations and claims shall be held illegal and void. The Congress shall have power to enforce by appropriate legislation the provisions of this article."

This amendment, as may be noticed, disfranchised nearly if not quite all the leaders of the South, and barred their way to office in state or Federal positions. But it did not guarantee suffrage to the colored population. It did affix a penalty for the denial of this right to them, but in many instances the South accepted the penalty, and rather than give the negro the privilege of suffrage, went to the extreme of surrendering their representation in Congress.

It was found necessary, therefore, to add still another amendment to the Constitution, which would declare the unconditional right of the negro to cast his ballot as any other American citizen. This is the celebrated Fifteenth Amendment, which was ratified by a majority of the States of the Union in 1870, and thus became a part of the constitutional law of this country. It is as follows:

"The right of the citizens of the United States to vote shall not be denied or abridged by the United States or by any State on account of race, color or previous condition of servitude."

There could be no evasion or misinterpretation of the plain, but brief, declaration of the right of suffrage contained in this Fifteenth Amendment. And now the colored race, vested with the unrestricted franchise, could, so far as the law was concerned, exercise the full and complete offices and privileges of citizenship.

I am free to admit that this Fifteenth Amendment was a radical measure, and attended at first with friction and danger, but what else could have been done? To have delayed the elective franchise would have been, perhaps, to defeat it for all time, and while the negro was not educated to the proper use of the ballot, it was better for him to use it even unwisely for awhile than never to have had it at all. I say that delay in conferring the elective franchise upon the negro would, in all probability, have been fatal to his hopes of citizenship, because I know the persistence and strength of race prejudice. Nothing but the ardor of patriotism kindled upon the altars of a bloody revolution, would have sufficed to have broken the shackles of this prejudice and set the negro free. The same spirit was yet alive when in 1870 Congress conferred upon the colored people of this country the full rights of American citizenship.

No one can deplore more than myself the misuse the colored man has often made and now sometimes makes of his ballot. Yet with all the abuse the colored man, and as to that, the purchasable white voters of this country, have made of this inestimable right of citizenship, I believe it would be a blow at the very foundations of American institutions to limit or in any way abridge that right. Education, when it has done its perfect work, will teach the colored man that his franchise is sacred, and that to prostitute or misuse it is one of the greatest crimes he can commit against God and his fellow-man. The white men of this country need to learn with their colored neighbors this same lesson. Example is contagious, and the negro is quick to imitate not only the

good, but the evil of his white brother. There is
no greater menace to free government than cor-
ruption in the use of the ballot, and all good men
should unite to condemn and extirpate this great
and growing shame by whomsoever practiced.

Heretofore political alignments in the South
have been determined by the race question. The
white people, as a rule, have voted with a party,
who, whether it be true or not, the negroes believe
is hostile to their interests and from which they
have thought they had little to hope. This attitude of the parties has tended to keep alive race
antagonisms and widen the gulf between them.
But the dawn of a new era is at hand. The
march of events has begun to invade the old alignments and Southern men are beginning to array
themselves as interest and not prejudice dictates.
This fact is full of promise to the negro and lends
hope to his political future. It augurs well for
the white man too. He will begin to feel more
kindness to his colored brother when he finds him
in the same political affiliations with himself, and
instead of trying to defeat his ballot he will use
every effort to make it effective.

As to State politics the colored man has long
since decided to use his best judgment and vote
for the best man irrespective of party. He recognizes the fact that his white neighbor owns most
of the property, and therefore must be vitally con-

cerned for good State and municipal government. As a rule the negro does not hesitate to vote for honest democrats in these local elections. This policy on the part of the negro has softened to some extent the extreme bitterness of the past and makes effective his ballot on all local issues.

When party prejudices shall be thoroughly set aside, and men in the South shall feel free from the party lash, as they now seem likely to do, a great stride will have been made toward harmony between the races. I have already alluded to the fact that many white people in the South are going over to the Republican party, and that Maj. McKinley, in the recent Presidential election, received thousands of former democratic votes. Maj. Hanson, a wealthy and intelligent manufacturer of Macon, Ga., whose social and moral standing is as good as that of any man in the South, has recently united with the Republican party. This step has given Maj. Hanson national prominence, and is notable as an indication of the disintegration of the Democratic party in the South. Hundreds of prominent and substantial men will follow his example, aye, have already done so. This change of front on the part of leading citizens in the South will continue to have a potent influence until the white people of the South will be divided just as are the white people of the North and West. Ward politicians may differ with me on this subject. It is natural for them to do so, as they make their living out of politics and are anxious to keep alive strife and party bicker-ings, but statesmen and philanthropists will view it as one of the hopeful signs of the times. Hon. Alexander H. Stephens, while a candidate for Gov-ernor of the State of Georgia, said to me: "I counsel you not to make too sharply the color line, for whenever it is distinctly made the whites, both North and South, will unite and the negro will be pushed to the wall."

The negro then has a vital interest in the politi-cal division of the whites. When this is accom-plished mere race issues will be left in the back-ground, and the great questions which are pressing for solution upon us as a whole people will be the issues upon which the great political parties of the country will divide, and about which they will contend.

# CHAPTER X.

## RECONSTRUCTION AND SUFFRAGE.

IT was natural that the Southern whites should have resisted reconstruction which involved negro citizenship and suffrage. They, like the Normans, were a haughty, hot-blooded race. Having held the negro so long in subjection, they could not brook the thought of his elevation to a position of equality before the law with them. It was indeed a severe blow to the gentry of the South, when the millions they had invested in slaves were swept away almost in a moment, and the fortunes of years scattered like leaves before the breath of the wind. I am just enough to say, that had I been a slaveholder, I would have felt the same chagrin and disappointment at the results of the war.

But in addition to the loss of his slaves, the slaveholder was now to witness the spectacle of those slaves elevated to citizenship and dignified with the ballot. This was indeed a bitter pill, and it was but natural that the Southern people should have been loth to take it. I for one was not surprised at the opposition of Southern whites to the reconstruction measures.

Led on by such distinguished orators as Benjamin H. Hill, of Georgia, Zebulon Vance, of North Carolina, and other leading men, the South resisted the adoption of the Fourteenth and Fifteenth Amendments to the Constitution with uncompromising animosity.

A few far-sighted statesmen of that section, such as Governor Joseph E. Brown, Senator Joshua Hill and Provisional Governor James Johnson, of Georgia, Ex-Governor James L. Orr, of South Carolina, and Horace Maynard, of Tennessee, advised the immediate acceptance of the situation, and had their counsels been followed, many of the evils of that period would have been averted.

It would be a thankless task to recount the dark days of bitterness and strife which make up what is called the reconstruction era. Feelings were engendered and prejudices created which have not passed away to this hour, and the colored man will long look back to that time as the darkest which marks the pages of his history since the dawn of his freedom.

The situation, however, was at length accepted. Even those who were at first the most hostile to reconstruction, became its warmest advocates. The Hon. Benjamin H. Hill, in 1870, wrote a letter to the people of Georgia, in which he said: "Reconstruction is an accomplished fact, and now that it is, let us accept it gracefully."

Several reasons influenced the South to accept Mr. Hill's advice, and to fall in line with the march of events.

First, the hopelessness of resistance. Negro citizenship and suffrage were but phases of his freedom, and this question, having been submitted to the arbitrament of the sword, was decided against the South. The South soon came to see that further resistance was not only futile, but kept alive a spirit of strife of which she was weary. When a question is settled right, resistance may be continued for a season, but will cease at length as reason and the sense of right come into play. When a question is settled wrong, resistance never ceases, and the verdict is eventually reversed and the question settled right. The South realized that it was but just that the negro should have his rights before the law as an American citizen, and the sentiment was so strong at last that resistance to it was hopeless.

Second, the South soon caught on to the advantage she would receive from accepting the Fourteenth and Fifteenth Amendments in national political affairs. Increased representation by reason of increased voting population, meant wider and more commanding influence for the South in the halls of Congress. The South realized suddenly, it seemed, that the negro constituted nearly one-half of her population, and that his legalized suffrage would almost double the number of her congressmen. This dream of power threw a quietus upon the opposition to reconstruction, and changed the attitude of the South from virulent antagonism into that of active, earnest championship of the measures of reconstruction. The Southern whites even took to a spirit of rejoicing over their good fortune, as they found that they could turn negro suffrage into a sort of boomerang and use it as a weapon upon those she deemed her political enemies at the North. This, indeed, acted as a powerful opiate on the spirit of resistance to reconstruction and led the South at length to become heartily in favor of it.

Third, especially did the Southern white people gladly accept reconstruction when it was discovered that by intimidation and fraud the negro's vote could be effectually disposed of. With the machinery of the State governments in their hands, it was easy to manipulate the ballot-box and either count it out or count it in to swell democratic majorities. Ballot-box stuffing for the first time came into vogue, and elections in the South were converted into the merest farces. The farce at length became so transparent and ill-disguised that the most ignorant saw through it, and the result was that the colored people soon ceased to vote at all. It is not surprising that the South, under these circumstances, came to actively champion reconstruction. So great a change in popular sentiment was rarely ever wrought in so short a time. Certainly there was a powerful reason for so radical a change of view, and that reason was an increase of representation in the legislative halls of the nation, based upon a constituency which could have no voice in the choice of that representation.

The Republican party at the North has recognized the status of the suffrage question as it relates to the negro at the South, but so far have been powerless to remedy it. Hon. James G. Blaine, in his address to the American people in 1884, attributed his defeat for the Presidency to the practical disfranchisement of the negro. He warned the North and the South of the dangers attending such political dishonesty and called upon good people, irrespective of sections, to unite against such methods.

It must be admitted by all fair-minded men, that such wholesale disfranchisement of a people, by illegal and high-handed means, is fraught with no good to either race. It is a standing menace to the integrity of free government, of which an untrammelled ballot is the corner-stone. It will educate the people in the processes of fraud and lawlessness, which will eventually rebound and react to the injury of the men and the parties who practice such methods.

I know that Southern whites have justified this

treatment of the negro, upon the ground that his vote is aimed at the best interests of the South, as they claim. They say the end justifies the means, and rather than submit to the influence of the negro in our political affairs, we will count out his vote altogether.

In reply to this specious argument, I will say that such reasoning would exclude from participation in the government and its affairs, not only every negro, but every Republican. Whenever and wherever the negro votes with the Democratic party, his ballot has the right of way, and will be counted. But if he prefers to vote the Republican ballot, it is not a fit ballot for a Democratic ballot-box, and is cast aside. This is generally, though not universally, true. Now, if the Republican party means harm and injury to the South, and Southern whites, the South could not be blamed for its attitude toward negro suffrage. But what are the facts? The most prosperous periods the South has known since the war, have been those in which the Republican party controlled in national affairs. The South is beginning to find out some things on these lines, and the tremendous support which Major McKinley received in the South for the Presidency is a significant and suggestive fact. If the Southern whites would cease to be solid because of the "negro question," or any other question, and join the good people of the North, or West, or East, on all measures that look to the good of the whole people, the sectional issue would be a thing of the past, and the conservative, law-loving, and liberty-honoring people of all sections would be united for the advancement and up-building of the whole country.

The time has come when men should vote their convictions. The "negro scare" is a myth. The colored people of the South do not wish to control or dominate the South. They recognize the fact, that virtue, intelligence, and wealth must rule the world, and the intelligent, sensible members of the colored race understand that the negro, like all other people, will advance to control and influence, only as these qualities of useful citizenship lift them up.

It is claimed that the South must remain solid, because of the negro. This is an unwarranted conclusion, based upon false premises. The negro is not a menace to the South. His natural sympathies are with the white man on all questions that look to the development and advancement of good government and a high civilization. Unlike the Chinese, the Japanese, the Italian, and the Pole, he has a fixed habitation. He is not in the South as a migratory denizen, ready to leave when he shall have acquired sufficient means to take him back to his native land. He aspires to be like his white brother, to imitate his progress, and to emulate his thrift and prosperity. His ambition is to become a sharer in his civilization, and to participate in the glorious destiny of Anglo-Saxon achievement.

Many white people believe that the negro hates the white man and distrusts him. I believe this to be wholly false. Even the wrongs of slavery have been well-nigh forgotten, and no race has ever so thoroughly confided their all to another as the negroes have to the white people of the South. The colored man loves his white brother, trusts him often to his own undoing, and would help him in his hours of distress and danger. In ten thousand ways the negroes of the South have shown their love for the white people. Not even suspicion generated by the memory of the olden times, and by the infliction of present injustice, has alienated his affection from his white neighbor at the South. They are naturally docile and friendly, and with kind treatment can be made the strongest ally the white man can have.

With a better understanding of the negro, the white people will not be so badly frightened at the "colored scare." They will then help rather than hinder him, and feel safe as his neighbor and friend. God grant that this era of friendliness and good feeling may speedily set in.

# CHAPTER XI.

THE negro was quick to see the necessity for education. Ignorant as he was, he seized the idea that his future was to be determined by the degree and extent of the enlightenment he should receive. The desire for knowledge amounted almost to a passion with him, and it was a matter of astonishment among the whites with what persistence and regularity he saw to it that his children avail themselves of all the opportunities afforded for their education. Everywhere the race encouraged the spirit of education, and welcomed the building of school-houses and the coming of teachers.

We have known of communities and have read of nations who resisted the incoming of knowledge. There are neighborhoods in the South among the whites who have as yet failed to observe the important part which education plays in the prosperity and upbuilding of men, and have made little or no provision for the instruction of their children. Missionaries to foreign fields tell us it is difficult to plant schools among the heathen which propose to teach nothing but general knowl-

99

edge. In China and Japan, until recently, a teacher was despised as much as a Christian missionary, the great masses of the people preferring "darkness rather than light." This opposition to the incoming of knowledge has been the greatest hinderance to the spread of the gospel among the millions of India and the islands of the sea.

This was not true of the negro. He not only tolerated the teacher, but greeted and welcomed him as the harbinger of good, as the bearer of light, as the publisher of good tidings. He longed to see his children have a chance in the race of progress, realizing as no other ignorant and illiterate race has, the necessity of knowledge.

History has failed to show a single instance of permanent progress and stability of any community or people who were ignorant and unenlightened. It is either knowledge or extinction, either progress or barbarism. The Roman was the master of the Gaul and the Briton so long as his civilization was superior. When the Roman receded in knowledge, and the Gaul and the Briton advanced, the Roman dropped back in the mastership of the world, and the Gaul and the Briton advanced to its conquest. England's sway, her wide territorial domain, exceeding that of Rome in her palmiest days, is attributed to the splendid enlightenment of her people. She rules the seas, and the sun never goes down upon her possessions, because behind her guns are enlightened freemen who conquer by the might of knowledge. Knowledge is power. It has been so in the past. It will be so in all the future.

I repeat it that the negro was swift to seize the idea of education. Nor has he abated one moment in his zeal for it, and, under difficulties that would have appalled a people less determined, can show a record in the educational statistics of this country of which he may proudly boast.

Even while the war between the States was still in progress, and before Appomattox had sealed the doom of the Confederacy and closed forever the chapter of slavery, the educational movement among the negroes began. Philanthropists from the North followed in the wake of the victorious Union armies, and found willing minds and hearts yearning for the boon of knowledge. Nothing in the history of the American negro redounds more to his lasting credit than this glad welcoming of light and learning. The joy of a newly-acquired freedom, the wild delight of the first moments of liberty could not blind him to his condition of ignorance, or induce him to neglect the means by which he was to convert his freedom into real and lasting benefit to himself and his children.

But few have taken the pains to inquire what was done on educational lines for and by the negro even during the progress of the war. Rev. J. L.

M. Curry, LL.D., secretary of the trustees of the
John F. Slater fund, furnishes some valuable in-
formation on this subject.  He says:

"Almost synchronously with the earliest occupation of any portion of the seceding States by
the Union Army, efforts were begun to give the
negroes some schooling.  In September, 1861,
under the guns of Fortress Monroe, a school was
opened for the 'contrabands of war.'  In 1862,
schools were extended to Washington, Portsmouth,
Norfolk and Newport News, and afterwards to the
Port Royal Islands, on the coast of South Carolina, to Newbern and Roanoke Island in North
Carolina.  The proclamation of emancipation, January 1, 1863, gave freedom to all slaves reached
by the armies, increased the refugees and awakened
a fervor of religious and philanthropic enthusiasm
for meeting the physical, moral and intellectual
wants of those suddenly thrown upon charity.  In
October, 1863, General Banks, then commanding
the Department of the Gulf, created commissions
of enrollment, who established the first public
schools for Louisiana.  Seven were soon in operation, with twenty-three teachers and an average
attendance of 1,422 scholars.  On March 22, 1864,
he issued General order No. 38, which constituted
a Board of Education for the rudimental instruction of the freedmen in the Department, so as to

'place within their reach the elements of knowledge.'

" Schools, previously established, were transferred to this Board, others were opened, and in December, 1864, it reported under its supervision 95 schools, 162 teachers, and 9,571 scholars. This system continued until 1865."

On December 17, 1862, Col. John Eaton was ordered by General Grant to assume a general supervision of freedmen in the Department of Tennessee and Arkansas. In the early autumn of that year, schools had been established, and they were multiplied during 1863 and 1864. His headquarters were first at Vicksburg, subsequently at Memphis. His assistant-superintendent reported, March 31, 1865, in and around Vicksburg and Natchez, 30 schools, 60 teachers, and 4,393 pupils enrolled. In Memphis, 1,590 pupils, and in the entire supervision 7,360 in attendance. These schools were taught, generally, by heroic women, who left their homes, and braved the perils of war to plant the seeds of light and knowledge in minds which had been long benighted. We have not space to record their names here, but they are written in the book of life.

Thus the first beginnings of the educational movement, for the benefit of Southern negroes, were at a time when war was desolating the land. In defiance of the laws of the Southern States, which had not yet been conquered, the colored people sent their children to school wherever and whenever they could. It is true that they did so only where the Union army was in possession of the country, but, amidst the varying fortunes of war, they were likely to lose the territory they had acquired, and often did. It took, therefore, no little courage to defy the legislation of the States, prohibiting their attendance upon schools, but neither the fear of the law, nor the poverty of their circumstances prevented them from supporting, as far as they could, and from patronizing, the schools, which were established by their Northern friends for their education.

To the white people of the North, who thus aided the colored race, not only to freedom, but to that education which was to prepare it for freedom, the negro owes, and will ever owe, a debt of gratitude. To General Grant, General Banks, Colonel Eaton, Secretary Stanton, and to all who founded and favored the first schools for colored people, we would ascribe all praise, and hold their names and memory in enduring reverence.

We have alluded to the fact that there were statutory laws in the Southern States prohibiting the education of negroes. These laws forbade meetings for teaching, reading and writing. The Nat Turner Insurrection in Southampton county, Virginia, in 1831, had alarmed the Southern people, and stringent laws were passed by the States, strengthening the prohibitions and penalties against education. Nevertheless, there were many good men and women in the South, who could not reconcile it with their consciences to keep their slaves utterly benighted. We record with pleasure the words of Hon. J. L. M. Curry, whom we have already quoted in another connection. He says:

"Severe and general as were these laws, they rarely were applied, and were seldom, if ever, enforced against teaching of individuals, or of groups, on plantations, or at the homes of the owners. It was often true that the mistress of a household, or her children, would teach the house-servants, and on Sundays include a larger number. There were also Sunday-schools, in which black children were taught to read, notably the school in which Stonewall Jackson was a leader. It is pleasant to find recorded in the memoir of Dr. Boyce, a trustee of the Slater Fund, from its origin until his death, that, as an editor, a preacher, and a citizen, he was deeply interested in the moral and religious instruction of the negroes. But, after a most liberal estimate for the efforts made to teach the negroes, still the fact exists that, as a people, they were wholly uneducated in schools. Slavery doomed the millions to ignorance, and in this condition they were when the war began."

We quote these words, not only to show that there were many good people in the South, who deplored the evils of slavery, and endeavored in some sort to mitigate them, but also to show that the negro was always ready and anxious to receive instruction, no matter by whom imparted.

# CHAPTER XII.

THERE were in this country in 1894, 61,000,000 whites and 8,000,000 negroes. The growth of the colored population has been phenomenal when we consider the conditions under which this growth has gone on. Mr. Bancroft, the historian of the United States, gives perhaps the most reliable estimate of the number of slaves in this country during colonial times. His estimate is as follows, beginning with the year 1750:

| | |
|---|---|
| 1750 | 220,000 |
| 1754 | 260,000 |
| 1760 | 310,000 |
| 1770 | 462,000 |
| 1780 | 562,000 |

A more reliable estimate is furnished by the records since 1780. Beginning with 1790 each succeeding decennial enumeration is shown in the following table:

| | |
|---|---|
| 1790 | 757,000 |
| 1800 | 1,002,037 |
| 1810 | 1,377,808 |
| 1820 | 1,771,656 |

107

| | |
|---|---|
| 1830 | 2,328,642 |
| 1840 | 2,873,648 |
| 1850 | 3,638,808 |
| 1860 | 4,441,830 |
| 1870 | 4,880,009 |
| 1880 | 6,580,793 |
| 1890 | 7,470,040 |

The white population in 1790 was 3,172,006, and in 1890 was 54,983,890. From this it appears that there were nearly eighteen times as many whites in 1890 as there were in 1790, and that the negroes were nearly ten times as numerous in 1890 as they were in 1790.

The whites have increased more rapidly for several reasons. First, their material condition was more favorable, having the benefits of superior clothing, food, shelter and the general physiological advantages which the conveniences and comforts of life secure. Second, the whites have had immensely the better of it in the additions which have been made to their numbers by the millions of foreigners which have flocked to America. Since the close of the slave trade in 1808 there has been but little addition to the colored population by immigration. They have increased in spite of these facts—the whites only about doubling them in the percentage of growth in the last one hundred years.

We may at least conclude from these figures

that the colored race is in no danger of extinction, and he who undertakes to consider the negro problem must leave this possibility out of the question.

But I am concerned chiefly in this chapter with the educational question as it relates to the negro. I propose to show that no race of people in any age ever rose so rapidly from absolute illiteracy—that no people who had been kept in bondage and ignorance for over two hundred years ever manifested such interest in their own enlightenment and uplifting. Happily for us the figures are at hand.

The Board of Education furnishes the following striking and suggestive table of the comparative number of white and colored children in the public schools of this country in 1876–77 and in 1891–92:

| Year. | Whites. | Colored. |
|---|---|---|
| 1876–77 . . . . | 1,827,139 | 571,506 |
| 1891–92 . . . . | 3,607,549 | 1,334,316 |

It is thus shown that while the number of white children in school in this country have nearly doubled since 1876–77, the number of colored children in these schools have more than doubled since that time. In other words, to quote from the Hon. J. L. M. Curry, LL.D., in 1876 the white pupils constituted 13.5 of the white population, and in twenty years this proportion increased to nearly 22 per cent. On the other hand the negro school children constituted in 1876 only 3 per cent. of all negroes, but in the same twenty years it has increased to nearly 20 per cent. of all negroes.

This evidently demonstrates that the growth of the educational spirit among the negroes has been more decided and rapid than among the whites, and the negroes should have credit for whatever there is of hopeful indication in these figures.

Dr. Curry further says, in "Statistics of Negroes in the United States": "In 1870, five years after they became free, the records of the census show that only two-tenths of all the negroes, ten years of age and over, in this country, could read and write. Ten years later the proportion had increased to three-tenths of the whole number, and in 1890, only a generation after they were emancipated, forty-three out of every one hundred negroes, ten years of age and over, were able to read and write. These figures show remarkably rapid progress in elementary education."

What suggestiveness and hopefulness in these figures? If education means progress and uplifting, then it would seem that the colored race is facing an era of gradual and healthy civilization. Of course, I do not contend that a mere elementary education is sufficient for these things, but when fifty per cent. of a people can read and write, and thus get into touch with the written thought of their own and of all times, they have the educational basis upon which to rise to high intellectual achievement and civilization.

The white race in the South can show little, if any, greater per cent. in the growth of elementary education. In some sections the percentage of illiteracy among the whites is even greater than among the negroes.

Now, all this progress on educational lines has been achieved under great difficulties. Among these we mention:

First, the extreme reluctance which any people, in the first years of their growth from illiteracy and ignorance to the rudiments of knowledge, have for the change. There is prejudice against education—a disposition among the ignorant to undervalue and discount learning. Ignorant parents say, "Let my children do as I have done. Work their way in the world as I have," and so they oppose and resist the education of their own offspring. As a people there has been less of this spirit among the negroes than perhaps among any people who were ever in like condition with them at the close of the war in 1865.

Again, many Southern whites opposed and discouraged the education of the negro. These contended that education was not desirable for the negro; that it would unfit him for the field and the workshop; that it would inflate him with pride, and make him a dangerous and vicious citizen. Teachers in many sections were discountenanced. White teachers for colored children were considered as favoring and practicing social equality, and their business deemed disreputable. The feeling was so strong, and is to-day, that few Southern white people could be induced to teach in negro schools, and the negro had to depend for teachers upon the few of his own race that were competent, and upon those who came from the North, willing to brave the Southern white sentiment and receive social ostracism at the hands of Southern people. I allude to these things with no feeling of resentment, but simply to show the facts of history, and how they operated against the efforts of the negro in his desire for education. This opposition of the whites to education for the negro, accounts, to some extent, for the fact that there was so little progress made in his education during the years immediately following the war, there being, in 1870, as we have already shown, but three per cent. of the colored people that could read and write. Gradually as the school got in its work, the supply of teachers increased, until at the present time there are a sufficient number of colored teachers to man all the public schools for colored people in the South.

The more intelligent white people at the South

soon became convinced, however, that education for the negro was not such a bad thing after all; that it did not operate to injure him as a laborer or a citizen, but, on the contrary, it improved and helped him in every way. Many distinguished and leading men, among whom we gratefully mention the late Bishop Atticus G. Haygood and Rev. Dr. J. L. M. Curry, began to plead for the education of the negro. The Southern States began to adopt the public school system, and for the first time public moneys were appropriated to common schools. In my own State, such men as Governor Joseph E. Brown, General John B. Gordon, Senator Alfred H. Colquitt and other leaders, looked with favor on the movement for popular education, and did much by their influence and names to remove the prejudice of the masses.

While this opposition of the whites retarded the movement in its earlier stages, I am glad to state that there is but little practical opposition to negro education by Southern white people at the present time. The leading men of the South favor it with tongue and pen, on the hustings and in the public prints. Ex-Governor Northen and our present governor, Hon. W. Y. Atkinson, have, time and again, gone upon record as the friends of negro education, pleading for a liberal policy upon the part of the State, not only in behalf of the education of the white, but also of the colored children of the state.

Still another difficulty was in the way of the education of the colored children of the South (and is still in the way), and that was poverty. Colored parents needed their children in the fields to help them make and gather their crops, or hired out as wage-earners to assist them in the support of others of the household. They could ill-spare their children from the cotton-fields. They could ill-afford to lose the wages which their labor brought to buy bread and clothing. It would be a chapter replete with pathos could it be written true to life, that recounted the sacrifices the ex-slaves of the South have made, and are still making, to educate their children. They subsisted on scanty fare, wore ragged and tattered garments, went without shoes often, and indeed denied themselves of all things, save the bare necessaries of life, that they might give to their children the advantages of the school. Mothers have worn their lives away at the wash-tub and the cook-stove to provide their children with food and clothing and books, that they might get the advantages of education. Fathers have toiled until they have worn themselves out in the cotton-fields and on the rice and sugar plantations of the South, to provide their children with the blessed boon of knowledge.

I might mention other causes which have operated against the negro in his efforts to secure education for his children. Many neighborhoods in the South are sparsely settled, and, as a consequence, the school-house was located at long distances from many of their homes. Many thousands of children have failed to get the advantage of school for this reason. Often, too, it has been difficult to secure a building of any sort adapted to the purposes of a school, and neighborhoods have been often put to it to provide suitable houses for this object. Many, too, have been too poor to buy books, and I have known of quite a number of instances of children being kept from school because their parents did not have the means with which to supply them with the books they needed.

And so we see that no race ever accomplished so much on the lines of elementary education in so short a time and in the face of so much oppositions and difficulties as the negroes have. Their educational history is indeed a miracle and a marvel of success under the discouragements with which they have wrought it out.

Surely there must have been deep down in the negro's heart a yearning desire for light and knowledge to have inspired him to make so many sacrifices, and to overcome so many discouragements in order to get these blessings. How he has triumphed is well proven in the immense army, now forty-three per cent. of all the race ten years and

over, that can read and write. Well may he be
proud of such a showing, perhaps unparalleled in
the annals of the race, when all the circumstances
are taken into the account.

With love and gratitude should the colored sons
and daughters remember their parents—some of
them gone to their reward—for the privations they
have suffered to secure to them the priceless blessing of education. Ah, how few appreciate these
sacrifices made in their behalf! How few honor
enough their living parents! How few cherish
the dust of those that are dead! Rather should
they rise up and "call them blessed," and crown
them with the unfading laurels of love and gratitude.

# CHAPTER XIII.

## CONTRIBUTIONS TO NEGRO EDUCATION.

THE efforts made for the education of the negro, during the Civil War, were necessarily tentative and spasmodic. Nothing like a general system of instruction could be put into operation even in those sections where the Union Army held possession of the country, though, as we have shown, a noble effort was made and much accomplished in the department of the Mississippi.

At the close of the war, or rather a few weeks before Gen. Lee's surrender at Appomattox, Congress created the Freedmen's Bureau. The acts authorizing this Bureau passed Congress and became the law, March 3, 1865. Large and comprehensive powers were granted to this benevolent institution; among others, it was authorized to promote education among the colored people emancipated by President Lincoln's proclamation, January 1, 1863. The commissioners of this Board were authorized and empowered to seize, hold, lease or sell all buildings and tenements and any lands appertaining to the same or otherwise formally held under color of title by the Confederate States, and buildings or lands held in trust for the same,

117

and use the same or appropriate the proceeds derived therefrom to the education of the freed people.

The Bureau was attached to the War Department, and Gen. O. O. Howard was appointed commissioner, with assistants. He was given almost unlimited authority and great liberty and scope of action. Within five years from the date of the organization of this Bureau, the school division reported the establishment of 2,118 schools, with 250,000 pupils. This Bureau was discontinued June 10, 1872. Of what was done by it during the last two years of its existence we have no means of ascertaining.

It is certain that this noble charity, inaugurated by the government, was the first great association which undertook to carry education to the colored people. This Board expended over $21,000,000 in charities during the seven years of its existence, but as to how much of this amount was appropriated to education there is no public report to show. Gradually the schools founded by this Bureau were turned over to the common schools, and merged into the educational system of the South.

We have stated that the Freedmen's Bureau was the first association inaugurated by the government for the education of the negro  While this is true, other benevolent societies antedated the Bureau. The teachers, earliest in the field, were from the American Missionary Association, the Western Freedmen's Aid Commission, American Baptist Home Missionary Society and the Society of Friends. After the surrender of Vicksburg and the occupation of Natchez, the United Presbyterians, the Reformed Presbyterians, the United Brethren in Christ, the Northwestern Freedmen's Aid Commission, and the National Freedmen's Association sent out teachers and money to aid in the education of the negroes in that department of the South.

The American Missionary Association was the chief body, apart from the government, in the first great movement that looked to the education of the negroes. The Freedmen's Bureau turned over a large sum of money to this society, which was to be used only in erecting and purchasing buildings. Since the withdrawal of several religious bodies from the association, in order to push their own educational enterprises among the negroes, it has continued to prosecute its church educational work with great zeal. It has now under its control—

| | |
|---|---|
| Chartered Institutions | 6 |
| Normal Schools | 29 |
| Common Schools | 43 |
| Attendance | 12,609 |

In 1866, was organized the Freedmen's Aid and

Southern Society of the Methodist Episcopal Church. Under that compact, powerful, well-directed and enthusiastic organization, more than $6,000,000 have been expended in the work of negro education. This church has sixty-five institutions of learning for colored people, 388 teachers and 10,100 students, and $1,905,150 worth of property, and $652,500 endowment.

After Appomattox the Baptist Home Mission Society was formally and deliberately committed to the education of the blacks, giving itself largely to the training of teachers and preachers. In May, 1892, it had under its management:

| | |
|---|---|
| Schools . . . . . . . . . . . | 24 |
| Pupils . . . . . . . . . . . | 4,861 |
| School Property . . . . . . . | $750,000 |
| Endowment . . . . . . . . . | $156,000 |

The Presbyterian Church at the North began to assist the course of negro education in 1865. From the twenty-eighth annual report of the Board of Missions for Freedmen it appears that besides building churches, exertions have been put forth in establishing academies, seminaries, and in equipping and supporting a large university. The report mentions:

| | |
|---|---|
| Schools . . . . . . . . . | 15 |
| Amount Expended . . . . . | $1,280,000 |
| Pupils . . . . . . . . . . | 10,520 |

The United Presbyterian Church reports, May, 1893, $2,558 in endowment for colored schools. The Southern Presbyterians have a theological seminary for the education of colored ministers at Tuscaloosa, Alabama.

The Episcopal Church, through the Commission on Church Work, during the seven years of its existence, 1887 to 1893, has expended $273,068 for the education of colored people. The reports do not give the number of teachers and pupils.

The Friends have done good work in the cause of negro education. They have sustained over 100 schools and have expended for this cause $1,004,129.

No man among the colored race has devoted more time, and thought, and labor to the cause of negro education than the late Bishop Payne, of the African Methodist Episcopal Church. He was a native of South Carolina, born in 1811. In 1865 he was called to the presidency of Wilberforce University, which institution he bought from the Methodist Episcopal Church without a dollar to make the first payment thereon. He raised the money by personal appeals to benevolent people all over the country, and finally turned it over to the African Methodist Episcopal Church free of debt. He is rightly called " the apostle of education." He led on his people in this great work and raised thousands of dollars to prosecute it.

He was to the colored people in the religious world what Fred Douglas was to them in the political world, and deserves to occupy one of the most exalted places in the history of his country and in the affections of his people.

The commissioner of education for the African Methodist Church has just published the following report, showing what that church is doing in the cause of secondary and higher education. Of course these schools get help from various sources, but the appended table will show the direction all moneys raised by and for the African Methodist Episcopal Church is taking. It is a splendid showing of what just one branch of the great Methodist family of colored churches is doing. As one of the official representatives of this church I feel a laudable pride in the following facts and figures:

Number of Teachers employed 167, Students 5533, Value of School Property $756,475.00, School Income for one year June 1st, 1895, to June 1st, 1896, $98,888.36, an increase over previous year of $17,342.46. The same ratio of increase being kept up for this present year will show an income for the year ending June 1st, 1897, of over $115,-000.00. (See table of schools attached.)

## OUR SCHOOLS FROM REPORTS OF 1896.

| NAME AND LOCATION. | Teachers. | Students. Male. | Students. Female | Students. Total. | Graduates. | Term Months. | Value of Property. | Debts. |
|---|---|---|---|---|---|---|---|---|
| Wilberforce University, Wilberforce, Ohio | 20 | 146 | 188 | 334 | 226 | 10 | $126,000 | $12,000.00 |
| Allen University, Columbia, S. C. | 6 | 144 | 160 | 304 | 208 | 8 | 50,000 | 10,500.00 |
| Morris Brown College, Atlanta, Ga. | 11 | 165 | 236 | 407 | 13 | 8 | 75,000 | 3,500.00 |
| Paul Quinn College, Waco, Texas | 6 | 60 | 50 | 110 | 32 | 9 | 70,000 | 9,000.00 |
| Edward Waters College, Jacksonville, Fla. | 4 | 48 | 53 | 101 | 8 | 8 | 25,000 | |
| Kittrell Institute, Kittrell, N. C. | 7 | 60 | 70 | 130 | 43 | 8 | 15,000 | 4,000.00 |
| Shorter University, Arkadelphia, Ark. | 4 | 28 | 40 | 68 | 5 | 8 | 5,000 | 1,400.00 |
| Payne University, Selma, Ala. | 4 | 88 | 97 | 185 | 12 | 8 | 5,000 | 300.00 |
| J. P. Campbell College, Vicksburg, Miss. | 3 | 55 | 52 | 107 | 13 | 9 | 35,000 | 574.00 |
| Western University, Kansas City, Kan. | 5 | 13 | 17 | 30 | | 9 | 75,000 | 2,000.00 |
| Turner College, Shelbyville, Tenn. | 6 | 28 | 52 | 80 | 65 | 9 | 1,200 | |
| Payne High School, Cuthbert, Ga. | 3 | 47 | 63 | 110 | 4 | 9 | 5,000 | 150.00 |
| Grant High School, Monticello, Ga. | 3 | 75 | 68 | 143 | | 8 | 700 | |
| Delhi Institute, Delhi, La. | 3 | 21 | 30 | 51 | 3 | 9 | 6,000 | 529.50 |
| Wayman Institute, Harrodsburg, Ky. | 2 | 18 | 34 | 52 | 3 | 10 | 4,500 | 962.10 |
| Fleger High School, Marion, S. C. | 2 | 70 | 82 | 152 | | 9 | 1,500 | 400.00 |
| District School, Rockmart, Ga. | 2 | 28 | 33 | 61 | | 8 | 1,000 | 50.00 |
| Price Normal School, Columbus, Ga. | 3 | 53 | 90 | 143 | | 9 | 3,500 | 200.00 |
| Harper Institute, Baton Rouge, La. | 2 | 16 | 32 | 48 | | 9 | 10,000 | 5,000.00 |
| Macon School, Macon, Ga. | 1 | 16 | 23 | 39 | 10 | 9 | 400 | |
| Davidic High School, Abbeville, S. C. | 3 | 80 | 130 | 210 | | 8 | 3,000 | 200.00 |
| Stringer Academy, Friar's Point, Miss. | 3 | 37 | 52 | 89 | | 9 | 3,600 | 325.00 |
| Salter Institute, Eastman, Ga. | 2 | 30 | 39 | 69 | | 7 | 300 | |
| Rosedale School, Rosedale, Ala. | 3 | 57 | 70 | 127 | | 8 | 800 | |

## OUR SCHOOLS FROM REPORTS OF 1896.—Continued.

| NAME AND LOCATION. | Teachers. | Students. Male | Students. Female | Students. Total | Graduates. | Term Months. | Value of Property. | Debts. |
|---|---|---|---|---|---|---|---|---|
| Dickerson Institute, Cartersville, Ga... | 1 | 28 | 40 | 68 | | | 400 | |
| McIntosh School, McIntosh, Ga... | 2 | 40 | 50 | 90 | | | 1,000 | |
| Camden District School, Snow Hill, Ala... | 2 | 50 | 70 | 130 | | 9 | 800 | 60.00 |
| St. James Academy, New Orleans, La... | 2 | 30 | 40 | 70 | | 6 | 5,000 | |
| Payne Theological Seminary, Wilberforce, Ohio... | 3 | 31 | | 31 | 14 | 9 | 14,477 | 8,296.00 |
| Sisson High School, Muscogee, I. T. | 3 | 30 | 45 | 75 | | 9 | 700 | |
| School, Vinita, I. T... | 1 | 10 | 13 | 23 | | 8 | 600 | |
| Johnson School, Eufaula, I. T... | 1 | 11 | 10 | 21 | | 8 | 700 | |
| School, Blue Creek, I. T... | 1 | 18 | 20 | 38 | | 5 | 75 | |
| School, Blue Pocket, I. T... | 1 | 4 | 6 | 10 | | | | |
| School, Brazil, I. T... | 1 | 14 | 16 | 30 | | | | |
| Atoka Schools, I. T... | 2 | 40 | 60 | 100 | | | | |
| Mossell School, Port au Prince, Hayti... | 6 | 80 | 100 | 180 | 8 | | 3,000 | 1,400.00 |
| Collegiate Institute, Hamilton, Bermuda... | 1 | 15 | 6 | 21 | | 10 | 600 | |
| Academy, Nassau, Bahama.* | 2 | 95 | 100 | 195 | | 9 | 300 | |
| Zion Institute, Freetown, Sierra Leone, Africa... | 4 | 167 | 143 | 310 | | 10 | 1,000 | 25.00 |
| Geda School, Freetown, Sierra Leone, Africa... | 1 | 81 | 99 | 180 | | 11 | 1,000 | 130.16 |
| Allen School, Magbelley, Africa... | 2 | 32 | 23 | 55 | | 11 | 20 | |
| Bethel School, Scarcies, Africa... | 1 | 20 | 11 | 31 | | 11 | 10 | |
| St. John's Maroon, Freetown, Sierra Leone, Africa... | 2 | 43 | 34 | 77 | | 11 | 600 | |
| Eliza Turner Schools, Monrovia, Africa... | 3 | 15 | 70 | 85 | | | | |
| Bethel School, Anna Catharina, W. C. Demarara... | 4 | 95 | 100 | 195 | | | 1,650 | |
| Virgenoegen, Demarara... | 2 | 13 | 17 | 30 | | | 500 | |

* From Report of last year,

# CHAPTER XIV.

## THE CAPACITY OF THE NEGRO FOR HIGHER EDUCATION.

YEARS ago it was popular and plausible to affirm the mental incapacity of the negro for anything like high civilization. Many of the whites believed his mission in the world was simply one of service to the higher and better endowed races; that he was created to be "a hewer of wood and a drawer of water." They even went so far as to maintain that there were ethnical and constitutional reasons which remanded him forever to inferior position in the great family of races. It was seriously argued by an anonymous writer under the signature of "Ariel," that the negro did not belong to the Adamic race at all, and was without a soul. These views were popular in the South at one time among a certain class.

For these reasons, especially, the contention that the negro was of inferior mental endowments, many were led to oppose all efforts looking to his education, and especially to his higher education. This hostility to the secondary or higher education of colored people is still kept up in many quarters, and it is seriously claimed by those who oppose it, that it is a waste of time and money.

As we have already shown, there are but few negroes of unmixed African blood in the South. Some of these, with black skins and kinked hair of the most pronounced type, have given evidence of intellectual power and capacity of marked degree. They have made orators, ministers, teachers, and even wise legislators, standing side by side with their Caucasian brothers.

But we are no longer dealing with a race of pure negroes, and it is no longer a question as to what an unmixed negro can accomplish in the matter of higher education, to what heights of learning he can attain, and how much knowledge he can appropriate. The question is, *now* what can a race of mixed white and African blood achieve? What can the Afro-Anglo-Saxon accomplish?

Take the view of our white brother for granted, and admit, for the sake of the argument, that the pure·negro is not susceptible of high intellectual culture. Then I reply, you have not touched the problem of higher education for the negro. You have worked it with an important equation left out, and the answer you have gotten is not one which follows from the "sum" given.

Can the negro as he is at present amalgamated, having both African and Indo-European blood in his veins, with the added factor that the Caucasian

element of blood is growing daily more widely distributed, and probably more rapidly infused from
new additions than ever before; can the negro so
constituted in this country, receive to any general
extent higher education?

To this question we unhesitatingly answer that
he is capable of any, even the highest education.
While this is the real problem, the practical question that is submitted we would insist upon, and
emphasize our belief in the highest possibilities,
even for the unmixed African under proper training and environments.

Now, what is this Afro-American race actually
accomplishing at the present time on the lines of
higher education?  The best proof of any proposition is the practical exemplification of it.  Figures and facts are conclusive, while mere theories
are often misleading and false.

Since 1876, speaking by the latest figures at
hand, $383,000,000 have been expended by the
States of this Union for public schools, and it is
fair to estimate that about $80,000,000 of this sum
has been expended for the education of the colored
children of this country.  In 1865 there were
practically no negroes that could read and write.
In 1870, five years later, and five years after they
were emancipated, the records of the census show
that two-tenths of all the negroes in the United
States could read and write.  Ten years later, or

fifteen years after they were set free, three-tenths of the whole number could read and write, and in 1890, or twenty-five years after freedom, forty-three out of every one hundred negroes that were ten years of age and over, could read and write.

A race so swift to rise from absolute illiteracy would naturally be supposed to be capable of advancing still further along the lines of higher education. And the facts demonstrate this in the face of difficulties which have seemed all along from a mere human view of the case to be insurmountable.

In the statistics, of the dates of 1893 and 1894, it appears that in the schools designed for the secondary or higher education of the colored people of this country there were 31,857 pupils. Of these 940 were in the colleges classes proper. United States School Commissioner Harris says, in the *Atlantic Monthly*, for June, 1892 : "It is clear that money expended for the secondary and higher education of the negro accomplishes far more for him. It is seed sown where it brings forth an hundred fold, because each one of the pupils of these higher institutions is a centre of diffusion of superior methods and refining influences among an imitative and impressible race. State and National aid, as well as private bequests, should take this direction first. There should be no gift or bequest for common or elementary instruction. This

should be left to the common schools, and all out-
side aid should be concentrated on the secondary
and the higher education."

These are the views of the most profound and
well-equipped authority on matters educational in
the United States. His opinions are accepted as
authoritative by the students of the educational
question in this country. In the words we have
just quoted, he not only assumes that the colored
people are capable of receiving higher education,
but maintains that money expended to this end
yields the far best results.

It is useless to multiply figures and authorities
to demonstrate a proposition which is being proven
every day by the number of graduates being
turned out from negro colleges, and by the larger
number who are receiving secondary education in
the schools which have been founded by the
bequests of philanthropic men in every section of
this country. Higher education is not only possible to the negro, but it yields the best revenues
to the race, in that it furnishes the teachers who
in turn become the "centres of diffusion of superior
methods and refining influences among an imitative and impressible race."

The fact being settled that the negro is capable
of receiving the higher education, and that education on these lines yields the largest revenues to
him in beneficial results, let us consider the impor-

tance of pressing it as widely as possible at this present time.

The same reasons that make higher education necessary to the best civilization among white people, make it so to the negroes. The intelligent whites are unanimous in their advocacy of the higher schools and colleges.

The colored people need it now, especially for the equipment of their ministry in all their churches. No one will dispute the proposition that an educated ministry is the proper ideal for the church of God. While I would not underrate or disparage the work of uneducated men in the pulpits of our churches, yet it would be irrational to attribute their success to the want of educational equipment. They have wrought a good work, despite the disadvantages under which they have labored. The pulpit needs and must have men in it who can intelligently expound the Scriptures and "rightly divide the word of God." The pulpit must be in advance of the pew—a centre of spiritual and intellectual light for the illumination of the hearts and minds of the hearers—else it will come to pass that the ministry will be composed of those who are "blind, leading the blind." I am aware that many of our so-called educated ministers have not measured up to the requirements of their sacred office; that, in many instances, they have been signal failures and have accomplished far less than their less advantaged brethren in the same calling. But this does not furnish an argument against an educated ministry, but must be chargeable to other sources of weakness found in the frailties of human nature, or the utter depravity of the heart of man. Educated men have been sometimes led into the responsible office of the ministry when they were not called of God to this work. Anxious and ambitious friends have persuaded them to assume these sacred duties, heedless of the fact that it is " God that willeth." Many, doubtless, with oratorical gifts and learning, have deemed the pulpit the best field for the display of these accomplishments, and have gone into the pulpit through vainglorious motives. These things account for the failure of some of our most cultured and scholarly men in the ministry. But let the educated ministry be truly set apart of God, and aglow with the zeal and fervor of the Holy Spirit, then will we see the greatest results wrought through religion and sanctified education for the enlightenment and salvation of men.

Not only do we need higher education for our ministry, but for our teachers, who are largely to mould the destiny of our race in this country for all time. The school-house is the manufactory where the civilization of a people is wrought. Here are born the aspirations of a race, here the tree is trimmed, and fertilized, and cultured, that is to bear the fruit of a nation's thought. Here the mind is lighted that is to shed the illuminating power of knowledge to the world. The schoolhouse is the birth-place of a nation's power, progress and civilization. How important then is the office of the teacher who presides over this little temple of the mind, this *plant* of the intellect, this *power-house* of the world! No ignoramus should be given rulership and authority here, but an educated, refined and intelligent brain capable of directing, controlling and illuminating. More than books, an educated man can communicate ideas, thoughts, culture. He is an incarnated library, a living book, a breathing intellectual force, from whom goes forth to the young committed to his charge not only the cold elements of knowledge, but the inspiring power of it, infused through the mind of the pupil like the glow from heated metal. We plead for a higher education because we want teachers for the negroes, not ignoramuses and know-nothings.

But we need higher education because we need cultured men in all the walks of life, and we know it is impossible to grow them in the soil of ignorance. We need representative men who can stand for our race in any coterie, on any rostrum, in any assembly. We have some of these, but we need multitudes of them, not only to demonstrate the capacity of the negro, but to furnish an inspiration to our people for knowledge. No man can estimate the influence even of a few cultured, intellectual men. Less than five hundred men created the magnificent wealth of Grecian literature. Less than a thousand names shine in the crown of England's literary glory, as yet unapproached in its richness by any other people ancient or modern. We as a race need the higher education that we may grow these great intellectual giants who shall illustrate the genius of our people by their triumphs on the thought-fields of the world.

I am not foolish enough to contend that higher education is now, or in the near future, possible to the great masses of the colored people of this country. I do not hope to confer this boon upon all of them, any more than I hope for it for the great masses of the white people. Perhaps, at this stage of the world's history, it is not best for all men. But, as Providence opens the way, we must be ready to furnish it to those whose circumstances and gifts render it possible and desirable for them to get it.

I will say that I rely upon this means, under the Gospel, as the greatest agency for the uplifting of the negro. Wealth and social elevation are bound up in the higher Christian education of our people. We are dreaming when we look for real progress and permanent improvement in any other direction. Let Wilberforce, Fisk, Roger Williams, Allen, Wiley, Livingstone, Waters, Morris, Brown, Clarke, Payne, Gammon, and all other colleges and universities of our church and of our sister churches, for the higher education of our people, go on in their grand work. Let them continue, on a wider scale even, to equip and send forth the men and women capable of standing abreast with the thought and culture of this age. Then will our people realize the power of educated, cultured leadership in our pulpits, in our schools, and in the social walks of life, to enlighten, elevate and save our race.

# CHAPTER XV.

THE negro, living for two hundred years in a state of servitude, learned the lesson of labor. He did not and could not learn the lesson of accumulation. All civilized nations have caught the Roman idea of private property, and much of their law relates to the titles and tenures by which private property is protected and held. This idea is at the foundation of all industrial enterprise and development, and is the motive for the creation of individual wealth which at last is the capital of a nation. Until a people get from under the burden of poverty on the one hand, and the communistic and patriarchal ideas of property on the other, national wealth is impossible.

The nations which have risen to empire in the world have been backed by wealth. Babylon, Egypt, Assyria, Persia, though poor beside the wealthy nationalities of modern times, were rich for that age of the world. Greece, Rome and Carthage had the wealth of the world at a later period, and these were the nations who moulded the destiny of the human race. This proposition holds good to-day. England's wealth is, and has

been, her defense. It was her money that saved
Europe from the grasp of Napoleon when all the
continental powers were exhausted and defeated.

The negro has no future if he is a failure in the
matter of accumulating property. If he has not
individuality sufficient to stimulate him to improve
his material condition, he had as well drop out of
the race for progress, and be content to be a
"hewer of wood and a drawer of water" for the
rest of time.

But is he a failure in this regard? Let us consider the matter briefly. I venture the assertion,
bold as it may seem, that no race in history, with
absolutely nothing to begin with, has in so short
a time accumulated as much wealth as the colored
people of America. Judge Albion W. Tourgee
said in his address to the Mohawk Conference in
1890: "They (the colored people) are better
economists than we are. They live with less expenditure than any equal number of white people.
A larger proportion of them have become land-
holders than of any equally impoverished and un-
prepared class of whites in a like period. A
smaller proportion of them are supported by public charity, a larger number of them have become
rich, and their aggregate possessions are greater
than any equal number of illiterate landless
whites, without inheritance or fortuitous discovery,
ever accumulated in twenty-five years."

From the most reliable authorities at hand, we find that the negroes of this country pay taxes on three hundred millions of property, and this has been invested over and above their living. They have made millions since the war, which have gone into the support of their families, their churches and their schools, and could they have been educated to soberness and economy, doubtless they could reckon as their wealth more than twice $300,000,000.

Three things are necessary before any people can accumulate great wealth. The first of these is education. No purely barbarous people have ever amassed wealth. China and India, with their millions of population, are poor, and will remain so until they are enlightened. When, therefore, we plead for education for the negro through the school and the church, we are pleading for the fulfillment of those conditions which will insure him a basis upon which he may build the super-structure of solid wealth for himself and his posterity. As he becomes more and more intelligent his desire for accumulation will increase. For education not only increases the capacity for wealth-making, but it increases the wants of men. As soon as enlightenment comes, the horizon of the mind is broadened, and man is no longer satisfied, like the untutored Indian with his bow and arrow and dog, but his desires widen, and reach out to lay tribute upon all things that may gratify them.

Go into the home of the educated, cultured colored gentleman, and there are beginning to be many of these in this country. It is no longer the dingy, squalid hut of former days, but a clean, sightly dwelling, with carpets and pictures, books, furniture, a well-supplied board, and all other comforts and decorations that make a neat, modern home. This is the outcome of education, as all must admit, and demonstrates how civilization in a short time may convert the slave of centuries into an intelligent, property-holding citizen.

Now, when we remember that this condition which is necessary not only to the capacity for wealth-making, but to the creation of the desire for property, has existed with the negro only about thirty years, it is indeed wonderful that he has accumulated so much. The facts seem to show that the negro, as a people, when educated, has the race faculty of acquiring property. Why not? There is no real difference between the wants of a negro and those of the white man. He has the same love of the beautiful in art and architecture, the same admiration for the elegant and tasteful appurtenances that embellish and decorate a modern ideal home, the same love of the comfort and conveniences that make such a home a delightful domicile, as his white brother. Educate him, refine his tastes, enlarge his aspirations, widen his mental horizon, and he will be found to be a successful wealth producer. If he has done anything toward his material improvement, it has largely come from the advantages of enlightenment, either directly through the schools, or indirectly through his contact with the intelligent Anglo-Saxon. Bishop Haygood stated in 1890, that there were at that time two millions and a quarter of colored people in this country who could read and write. Here is the partial explanation of the fact that the material condition of the colored people has so rapidly improved.

The second condition of wealth is industry. No indolent people have ever accumulated great wealth. God has fixed the law that nothing valuable can be secured without labor, and no nation can grow in an industrial and commercial sense without conforming to this law.

The charge has been made that the indolence of the negro is an effectual barrier against his accumulating wealth. It is said that he is a lazy, sluggish, phlegmatic being, without sufficient energy to succeed on the lines of material progress. How baseless such a charge in the light of his history during slavery and since emancipation. It was his labor that created the wonderful wealth of the South before the war, which was at that time the richest section of the Union. Since emancipation, he has shown himself no sluggard. His brawn and muscle largely produce the 9,000,-000 bales of cotton the South is now annually pouring into the markets of the world. The Southern landholder prefers him for a tenant to any laborer he can get, and hundreds and thousands of acres are turned over to him for cultivation. Wherever hard work is to be done, in the field, in the shop, in the building of railways, roads or cities, the colored laborer is in demand. With some show of truth, the negro may be charged with the want of proper economy in the saving of the products of his labor, but not with indolence. Intelligence and experience will do much in working a reformation in him in this regard, and the time is not far distant when his earnings will be converted into real and permanent wealth.

The third condition of a people's wealth is personal liberty. The colored people received political freedom more than thirty years ago. Of course they could not amass property for themselves before. But since their freedom, while ostensibly and politically free, the largest liberty has never been theirs. The negro has never been permitted to enter unrestrained into free and full competition with his white brother in the South. There are many avenues of employment from which he is shut out. In railway service he is allowed to fill no place above that of porter in a sleeping-car. He is not employed as conductor, engineer, car inspector, passenger or freight agent. He is not wanted as a clerk in any mercantile establishment, as agent for insurance companies, as bank clerk, or indeed in any lucrative place in any branch of business. The places reserved for him are the menial places or the places requiring muscle and sinew, and yielding the smaller pay. Even in politics the fat plums go to his white neighbor, and he must take what is left. Even the learned professions—law, medicine, professorships in colleges, unless it be a school for colored people—are practically closed against him. These fields of enterprise are almost wholly pre-empted by white men.

Yet, notwithstanding the restraints put upon him and the limitation of his sphere of activity, he has gone on and amassed more wealth than any people ever similarly situated; aye, more than any people, no matter how situated, in the same length of time, who started with nothing. How long these limitations will continue are questions which will be decided by another, and that is, How long will it be before the negro shall be as highly educated as his white brother?

There are no ethical or racial reasons why the colored man may not reach an independent position in his economic life. Even the prejudice of color and caste will pass away when education and moral training have done their perfect work. As yet the cotton fields and the sugar and rice plantations of the South have been almost the sole avenues of honorable wealth open to the negro or the South. Even here he is showing himself to be a property-maker, a wealth-producer. As he advances in intelligence, his theatre of honorable enterprise will widen and he will abundantly demonstrate his capacity to succeed on all lines, even the highest.

# CHAPTER XVI.

## MARRIAGE—HOW REGARDED.

PRIOR to 1865, there had never been a legal marriage among the negroes in the South, and hence, before the law, every colored person in that section was a bastard. Civil marriage among colored people was not provided for by statute. The negro had no civil rights under the codes of the Southern States. It was often the case, it is true, that the marriage ceremony was performed and thousands of couples regarded it and observed it as of binding force, and were as true to each other as if they had been lawfully married. But, as a matter of fact, no marriage was legal and no colored child was legitimate until after the war. Then it was that laws were enacted by all the Southern States, making legal all unions of ex-slaves who had lived together as reputed man and wife prior to that time, and providing for the legal marriage of all who should enter the state of wedlock subsequently to the passage of said law. It will always be to the credit of the colored people that at most, without exception, they adhered to their relations, illegal though they had been, and accepted gladly the new law, which put the stamp of legitimacy upon their union and removed the brand of bastardy from the brows of their children.

The colored people generally held their marriage (if such unauthorized union may be called marriage) sacred, even while they were yet slaves. Many instances will be recalled by the older people of the South of the life-long fidelity and affection which existed between the slave and his concubine—the mother of his children. My own father and mother lived together for over sixty years. I am the fourteenth child of that union, and I can truthfully affirm that no marriage, however made sacred by the sanction of law, was ever more congenial and beautiful. Thousands of like instances might be cited to the same effect.

Giving my people due credit for whatever progress they have made, the fact still remains that the marriage relation is too lightly regarded and too easily thrown off among them at the present day. This is true of the white race also, especially in the cities and the more densely populated districts. This has been with the negro, one of the incidents which has resulted from the sudden acquisition of freedom, and which I am charitable enough to believe, was inseparable from the low condition of intelligence in which he has groveled. In abject poverty, without money or habitation, want and deprivation have driven him sometimes to abandon his family to avoid the responsibility of providing for them. These things are not offered as excuses, but as explanatory of the seemingly loose views which obtain among many in regard to the sacred institution of marriage.

But I must not be too lenient, nor must I overlook or misinterpret the facts in dealing with this vital question. Poverty and ignorance play their part in bringing about laxity of marriage vows, but the want of a high sense of honor is the bottom fact in most cases of ill-fated marriages and ruined homes. Nor is the blame always to be attached to the colored husband. I am not gallant enough to mistake the facts nor blind enough to fail to see them. The colored women of the South, though not to the same extent, must share with their husbands the responsibility for this state of things. It is often the case that by failing to be a "keeper at home," and to preserve herself chaste and pure, she forfeits the love and respect of her husband, and this renders his marriage distasteful and repulsive. If she is a woman of personal comeliness she is exposed to the lust of the immoral white man, who with money may lure her, if she be susceptible to such influence, from the path of virtue and honor. These are painful facts which it were criminal to overlook, and bear directly upon the question of the marriage relation of the colored people of the South. At this point, as at all other points vital to the negro, the white man touches the social life of the colored people. The growing looseness of the marriage relation among white people has its reactionary effect upon the imitative mind of the negro, and he follows the bad as readily as he does the good example of his white neighbor and brother.

These observations force me to admit with sorrow that there is not that high regard for marriage among the colored people of America which should characterize all self-respecting people, being, as it is, at the foundation of all social elevation and home happiness and purity. Some reflections, therefore, relating to reformation on this line, will be apposite and germane.

1st. As a race we invoke the aid of the civil law in the proper enforcement of the marriage institution. Husbands should be compelled, as the law provides, to care for and maintain their wives and children. A man has no right to bring innocent children into the world and then abandon them to the charities of the world for bread and raiment. The law should not tolerate divorce except for Scriptural cause, and make, as it does now, the escape from matrimony an easy process. The records of divorce courts show an alarming state of things both among white and colored. The safety of society, the sanctity of marriage, the integrity of the home, the preservation of virtue, all alike demand that our civil law should guard the marriage institution with a zealous eye and a strong hand.

Education on the line of the family, a necessity of civilization, should be taught in our schools and preached from our pulpits. Let our people know that when you tamper with the marriage relation, you are an enemy to God and to society; that when you dismantle the home and break down its altars, you tear away the pillars of liberty and raze the temple of civilization. Here it is that children are to breathe the atmosphere of love, and reverence, and truth, and purity, which mould them for the highest citizenship. Here it is if the home is well ordered and regulated, the youthful minds and hearts are to get from wiser heads that instruction in righteousness and that inspiration of knowledge which are to prepare them for usefulness in subsequent life. That man, be he white or black, is a dastard and a fool when he tampers with the sanctity of the home or lends himself to the destruction of the marriage institution, which is its condition and foundation.

Not only is the social future of the colored race bound up in the marriage relation, but his religious life is also. Aborted marriages, unscriptural divorces, go to the very heart of the spiritual life of a people. The Bible lays its greatest stress on the home. Christ entered the homes of the common people, and forever glorified honorable marriage and the consecrated home. The church of God is dreaming if she imagines that she can go forth to permanent and real prosperity over the broken altars and sundered marriage vows of her false and dishonoring membership. He is a faithful minister who illustrates in his own life his sacred estimate of the marriage vow, and who stands like Nathan of old for chastity, whether in the king or in the most humble peasant. Religion at last is the only prop of virtue, and in turn virtue is the only prop of religion. A church filled with adulterers and adulteresses is but a repetition of that assemblage against which the Saviour of the world uttered the most awful anathemas that ever fell from the lips of God. Hear also the words of the apostle James, whose fidelity to God and his truth crowned him with the honor of martyrdom: "Ye adulterers and adulteresses, know ye not that the friendship of the world is enmity with God." Of all people on earth, it seems to me the negro should stand for those principles which are vital to religion. Gratitude to God, who so marvelously broke from his feet and hands the shackles of bondage, should ever prompt him to render to that God the homage of his heart and the devotion of his life. If thus he would evince his love and gratitude, let him see to it that His law relating to marriage shall be observed and perpetuated forever.

I know of no nobler work to be achieved by and for the negro than that of strengthening among them respect for the marriage institution. We prate of liberty and boast of progress, but these are a delusion and a snare if we allow the altars of home to be desecrated and our household gods to be removed.

The colored people who have any real position, who command the respect of those whose respect is to be desired, are those who magnify marriage and regard the home. Thank God there are many of these whose homes though humble are sacred shrines which they love and honor and protect. Here they cherish their wives, rear to useful life their children, and worship God in the beauty of holiness. God be praised for such examples and illustrations of true manhood and womanhood, for such specimens of Christian character and citizenship.

Let every good man among us help to create and foster a sentiment that will not tolerate marital infidelity. A man who deserts his family, his wife and helpless children, ought to be placed in penal servitude until he learns to abide with them and give them the means of living. A wife who is untrue to her husband, or deserts him for insufficient cause, ought to be ostracised from good society, and thus taught that no faithless wife shall be respected.

I would stress and emphasize the views set forth in this chapter. I feel that they are of vital interest to my people. If we rise to honorable, respectable life, to desirable place and position among the great family of peoples, we must, by every token, insist upon and demand the observance of the marriage law and the marriage relation, and thus put the world upon notice that we stand for social purity. family honor and home preservation.

# CHAPTER XVII.

## AMALGAMATION.

MUCH has been said and written on the subject of amalgamation. It has been the consummation which some have so much dreaded. Yet if its accomplishment is at last to be recorded, it will be the work of that race which has so persistently fought it.

Many have claimed that there are but three destinies possible to the negro, viz, extinction, emigration and amalgamation. The American Indian has been pointed to as a proof of the extinction theory by those who offer it. They point to him to show that no race which is not a cognate race, can exist side by side with the Anglo-Saxon. Alas, for this theory, the facts furnished by the latest statistics show that the negro, instead of dying out, is increasing with wonderful rapidity.

The emigration theory has been found to lack practicability. The negro does not take to it, in the first place, and if he did, it would be hardly possible to put it into effect. The difficulties involved in such a scheme, whether it be colonization on a foreign shore or in some neighboring state, are well nigh, if not altogether, insurmountable.

The amalgamation theory is the only one of these which has a basis of probability. While I am in favor of preserving the racial integrity of my people, and deplore miscegenation in all its phases, I am not blind to the fact that amalgamation is no longer a theory, but well-nigh an accomplished fact; and if the interblending of the races keeps up in the same ratio it has gone on in the past, it will be totally consummated in the not distant future. The African negro will no longer appear as a factor in American civilization, but in his stead will be the mulatto, the product of mixed white and colored blood.

According to the statistics of the United States, for 1890, there were about one million and a quarter of mulattoes in the South. These do not include the multitudes who have traces of white blood in their veins. Indeed, except in remote sections, it is difficult to find a negro of unmixed African blood in the entire Southern country.

Thus it appears that the dreaded amalgamation is already partially accomplished. It no longer belongs to the realm of theory; it has been transferred to the region of fact. Silently, and in defiance of law, this interblending of races has been going on for years, until, like leaven, it has well-nigh leavened the whole lump.

These may be unpleasant and unpalatable truths both to the better class of white people and negroes, but they are truths nevertheless, and cannot be overlooked or set aside in any intelligent consideration of the negro question.

Let us discuss some of the causes which have contributed and are still contributing to bring about this result.

1st. The exposure to which colored girls are subjected. Protection, afforded by well-ordered homes, is necessary to the preservation of virtue among any race or any people. The poverty and ignorance of the colored people have made them largely a homeless people. They and their children must toil by manual methods for their physical sustenance. At an early age colored girls are hired out to help make the revenues, which must be had for the support of the family. Thus exposed and unprotected, they become the easy prey of the white man, whose love of virtue is not strong enough to deter him from despoiling the young and unsophisticated colored girl. Exposed in this way it is not long before she becomes an adulteress and a mother, and the child of mixed blood comes into the world.

2d. Ignorance. Ignorance has many sins justly laid at its door, none of which is blacker than that of fornication and adultery. No ignorant people, I care not how they may boast of chastity, can preserve even the semblance of virtue when they come into contact with a more refined and intelligent race. Intelligence and money, unrestrained by moral principle, will debauch any race less intelligent and less affluent. The American Indian has been cited as an illustration of an ignorant yet virtuous race. It is a notorious fact that whenever he is civilized enough to remain in contact with the white man for any length of time, the result is a multitude of mixed breeds. There must be intelligence if there be chastity. Who but the cultivated and refined can properly estimate the value of purity? Ignorant and untutored, the average colored girl goes out to the tempting and seductive influences of an exposed life, and thousands there are to bid for her ruin. And so she is swept off into the current of vice to land at last on the rocks and reefs of husbandless motherhood. While this is true, on the other hand, with those girls who have been properly trained and educated in well-guarded and protected homes, virtue and chastity are as highly prized as with any similar class of any race.

3d. Moral and religious deprivation. Proper home protection and education are powerful factors that enter into the question of the personal and social purity of the women of any race, but these are insufficient. It takes the additional element of religion to form the mighty bulwark which guards the portals to virtue and personal honor. Let reverence for God and His law take deep hold upon the conscience and the moral nature, then you have the highest incentive to right living that ever actuated a human being. But as a race the colored people have been deprived of such moral training and instruction. Thirty years ago, but five per cent. of the race could read and write. They had no access to books or written instruction of any sort. The Bible itself was a sealed book, and the little instruction they received was second-hand. So they were not only ignorant, and weak by virtue of their ignorance, not only exposed and temptible by reason of their exposure, but they were without a moral conscience and were weakest of all at this point, on account of the lack of this conscience. These causes are still operating, though in a diminishing degree, and will continue to operate so long as these conditions exist.

4th. Another cause which has contributed to the amalgamation of the races, and which is the result of the causes already stated, is the premium which the negro himself puts upon white blood. I say it to the shame of my people. Colored girls in the South often prefer to be the mothers of white children. The white skin and straight hair are possessions to be admired, and instead of being ashamed of the disgrace of which such marks are the evidence, they are proud of them, and boast-

fully flaunt them to the world and before the eyes
of their own race. With such ideas it seems a
hopeless case. The girls with light skins and
straight hair, too, are preferred for wives by colored men and youths to the women of pure African descent. With such manifest preference for
amalgamation, and with such conditions to forward it on, is he a dreamer who predicts its final
consummation?

5th. Nor are the causes underlying this rapid
miscegenation confined to the conditions which
apply to the negro race alone. It takes two to
make a bargain of any sort, and emphatically one
of this kind. There is a growing indisposition on
the part of the young white men of the South,
and as to that, in many other parts of the world,
to marry and assume the responsibilities of families. With access to so many colored girls they
prefer to live in license and shame rather than take
upon themselves the burden of rearing children in
honorable marriage. The white man who does
not hesitate to use violence toward a colored man
for illicit intercourse with a white woman, even
with consent, does not scruple to live in adultery
with a colored woman. Nor is this adulterous intercourse confined to the young unmarried men of
the South. It is common for married men to have
their colored concubines, and to raise up children
by them in the same towns and communities

where their legitimate families reside. The white man is thus seen to be the potent factor in this ever-growing evil, which threatens the speedy interblending of races in the South. By reason of superior wealth and advantages he is in position to carry on this process of miscegenation, and when it is at length accomplished, the sin of it must lie chiefly at his door.

As I have already stated, I am opposed to miscegenation and all means which are used to accomplish it, and would remove, if I could, the conditions which make it possible.

There are evils connected with this whole question of amalgamation which ought to be stressed.

First. Amalgamation under the laws of the Southern States is possible only through adultery and fornication. The law forbidding the intermarriage of the races renders every child so born a bastard, and its mother an adulteress. Begotten under such illegitimacy, the child must go through the world with the brand of bastardy upon his brow, and its mother must wear the scarlet letter upon her bosom. This is enough to mar the future of both. The subjective influence of such sin upon the part of the parent, and such humiliation on the part of the child is deleterious in a high degree, as it operates to the destruction of that fine sense of virtue and chastity which are the chief qualities of a self-respecting people.

The whites readily observe the blighting influence of such illegitimacy, and the very laws of the country incorporate the proscription which the civilized world has meted out to the unfortunate offspring of illegalized intercourse. Let this evil of illegitimacy be widespread; not limited to individual instances, as is the case with the white people, and the magnitude of the evil can be partially calculated. Take the child born under such relations. Branded with bastardy, going forth without recognized parentage, he carries with him the consciousness of his tainted birth, which, if he be human, must wound his pride and fester like a wound in his bosom. Amalgamation without legitimacy is a blight upon both mother and child, an unnatural and a divinely forbidden crime against God and society.

Second. It is far-reaching in its immoral effects, cursing not only those who are the direct subjects of it, but menacing to those who behold it. It is a standing threat to the virtue of the race, a sword of Damocles which hangs suspended above the chastity of every daughter of the negro in the South. Those who behold it are in danger of it. The child sees (for such things cannot be hid) the illicit relations of her mother with a guilty paramour, and at length becomes familiar with sin. So the poet expresses the thought—

Vice is a monster of such hideous mien
That to be hated needs but to be seen;
But seen too oft, familiar with its face,
We first endure, then pity, then embrace.

Thus, we see, that the demoralizing influence of unlawful amalgamation permeates through every strata of colored society and saps the virtue of the race, like poison from the bite of a serpent, which slowly infuses itself through every part of the system, until it reaches and stills the heart itself.

Third. The effect of amalgamation is to discount and put at a disadvantage the negroes of unmixed blood. Mulattoes have the preference, even in the eyes of the whites, and, as a rule, their light skins give them choice of positions in the better employments open to negro labor in the South. In the hotels, on the railway cars, as servant girls, in the homes of the rich, the light skin is the winning card, and the black-skinned negro is elbowed off to more menial labors, which require nothing but sinew and muscle. It has even come to pass that many believe the pure negro incapable of any high degree of civilization, and the evident progress of the colored race since emancipation is attributed by these to admixture of white blood in their veins. The white man, as a rule, is not disposed to reason, like the Irishman who heard Fred. Douglas speak. When told that he was a half negro, he said: "Well, faith, if he can do so well as a half-negro, what could he do if he was a whole one?"

Thus, it will be seen, that amalgamation as partially consummated already, and as in still further process of accomplishment, operates at least, in our time, to the detriment of the colored people in various ways. If Providence means by this process to solve the negro question, it would be a futile task to oppose it. But I cannot lend myself to the belief that God gives his sanction to evil, even though it be that good will eventually come out of it. I know that Providence has often overruled sin and diverted its results into the channels of good. The adulterous and violent conduct of David, which ultimated in his union with Bathsheba, had, as its final outcome, that genealogical product, Christ, the Saviour of men; but the sin, from which such good came at last, was paid for by the life-long penitence and punishment of the criminal himself. So if amalgamation, in the most hopeful view of it, means the ultimate good of our race, those who practice it now must pay for their sin by their own prostitution, and by the abasement and moral defilement of their immediate offspring.

# CHAPTER XVIII.

## THE INTERMARRIAGE QUESTION.

THERE is but one instance in the history of the world of race persistence where intercourse with other races was free and unrestricted. The Jews have maintained their ethnical identity more perfectly than any other people who have come into contact with other peoples. Yet with all their boasted purity of blood, it must be admitted that admixtures have taken place.

The African, or negro, is no exception to the general law of amalgamation. Ethnologists tell us that the interblending of races is favorable to the general progress of mankind. It is certain that the Anglo-Saxon is a composite race. He has several strains in his blood. First, that of the ancient Briton, which was purely Celtic; then a slight infusion of the Latin or Roman, which he received during the four hundred years when Rome occupied Britain as a conquered province. Then the Teutonic strain, which he received from the German conquest under Heugist and Horsa. Then the Scandinavian or Norman infusion of blood resulting from the conquest of England by William the Conqueror in the year 1066. The

Anglo-Saxon race is thus seen to be a composite race, and this is its pride and boast.

It is true that the interblending of races has been more decided among some tribes or races than others. This is dependent upon the opportunities for intercourse with other people. The American Indian, until recently, and many Asiatic and African tribes have kept their racial integrity for thousands of years owing to their isolated geographical and commercial situation.

The negro in America has, as has been stated, been in process of amalgamation for all the years of his residence in this country. This amalgamation has gone on under the most unfavorable conditions, despite law and a public sentiment which at least affected to condemn and discourage it. It has gone on until the best and most discriminating observers in the South affirm that there are not left but two millions of pure unmixed Africans out of the more than eight millions of this race in this country.

In the light of these facts, is it rational to suppose that the American negro will continue a negro? Is it not inevitable that in the course of time he will lose his distinctive color and become practically a Caucasian? The fact, as we have shown, is already partially accomplished, and every present indication points to its total consummation in the process of time.

I am and have ever been opposed to amalgamation. I believe that the negro has the inherent racial capacity for high achievement—that under proper conditions the unmixed African can reach the summit of intellectual and moral excellence. Some of the most splendid specimens of physical and intellectual manhood I have known were unmixed Africans. There is no ethnological reason why the negro may not reach the highest material and intellectual civilization if his environments could be favorable.

But so far as the negro in America is concerned, it is impossible now to make the experiment. The unmixed African, as we have stated, constitutes but a small proportion of the American negroes, and the proportion will grow smaller as the years pass away.

Painful though these facts may be, we must look them in the face and deal with them as we find them. While I would arrest further amalgamation, I know such a hope is chimerical. There is almost enough white blood coursing the American negroes' veins to-day to Caucasianize the whole race without further admixture if that blood were generally distributed.

This being the state of the case, many people even in the South, and at most, all the people of the North, favor the undoing of all legislation forbidding the intermarriage of the races. Mrs.

Edna D. Cheney, in the Mohonk Conference held at Lake Mohonk, Ulster County, New York, June, 1890, voiced the almost unanimous sentiment of the North when she said:

" I believe that we are bound to brush away all barriers that separate the negro from the white man. I do not know whether the sexual amalgamation of the races is desirable or not, but I do believe that every law forbidding intermarriage should be swept from the statutes. If it is a law of nature that they should not mingle, leave it to nature, and nature will work it out, but every refusal to legalize marriage is to give opportunity to illegal and irregular unions."

This is the language of one of the most cultured and highly respected women of the North, and as we have before stated, is well-nigh the universal sentiment of the largest section of this country.

While there may be some plausibility in these views, I cannot lend myself to the advocacy of intermarriage between the white and negro race. I cannot believe it is best to encourage by law rapid miscegenation.

First, I desire to preserve as long as possible the integrity of my race. I for one am proud of my blood, and I would not help to adulterate it legally or otherwise. I would like to see, hopeless as the complete experiment seems to be, what my

race could accomplish under its present civilizing
environment, at least without total absorption into
the white race. It is natural that any human being should resist a process that means the extinction of the race to which he belongs. I have that
pride of race which would make me desire to preserve it intact and unadulterated, and observe its
march to worthy and noble achievement without
the aid of foreign blood. I believe that the negro
needs only the uplifting power of knowledge and
religion to make him the peer of any race. It is
a mistake to suppose that he has no innate aspiration, no capacity for great things.

Will the reader pardon a personal allusion?
When I was a child I was the property of Mr.
Gabriel Toombs, a brother of Gen. Robert
Toombs, the great Southern orator and statesman,
one of the most splendid specimens of physical
and intellectual manhood my eyes ever beheld. I
would frequently see General Toombs, and Hon.
Alexander H. Stephens, and Bishop George F.
Pierce, all peerless orators, at the home of my
owner, and I always felt the inspiration of their
presence. I was conscious that there was something in me that made me aspire to be what they
were. I felt that if I could be loosed from the
bonds of slavery and have the liberty of an unrestrained life, I could rise to be something and
somebody in the world. What a mistake, there-

fore, is made when others of a different race suppose that the negro is incapable of those high aspirations which make possible a full rounded manhood. I for one would like to see the experiment made with a race of pure Africans, into whose veins had come no foreign strains of blood.

But I am opposed to intermarriage between the white and colored races, because if in any event or at any time it were desirable, the time is not yet, nor has there yet developed, so far as I can see, any good reason for such legalized interblending of the races. The intense prejudice of the whites in the South would render such legalized miscegenation a source of constant friction, and I believe those who would dare to practice it, even under statutory law, would be in peril of their life. We are not wanting at this time any legislation that would tend to irritate and excite strife. It is the policy of the colored people, as well as their desire, to live in peace and harmony with their white brethren, and in my judgment nothing would so excite the animosity of our white neighbor as the agitation of legalized miscegenation.

Finally, I am opposed to the intermarriage of the white and colored races, because my own people are opposed to it. The intelligent and educated people of this country are not seeking intermarriage. They do not want it. They are seeking for that kind and respectful treatment which the most insignificant foreigner receives, provided he is a white man. The law-makers,who are responsible for the legislation which discriminates against the colored man for fear that he may aspire to intermarriage with the whites, is doing him a great injustice.

I am opposed to the agitation of the whole question. The subject is a delicate one, and does not need to be discussed, and I allude to it only to oppose any radical views that may be entertained by the people of my own color. This, like all other questions, will solve itself in the run of the years. I have considered it as delicately as possible, and would offend no one of either race by the views I have advanced.

# CHAPTER XIX.

## THE POLITICAL QUESTION AND THE NEGRO.

THE negro population of this country now numbers more than 8,000,000. Of these about 1,500,000 are voters. If that vote could be fairly registered it would be a telling factor in the National and State elections of this country.

Many have inquired why it is that the negro has always affiliated with the Republican party. The question may be answered in a few words. It is because the Republican party originated the anti-slavery agitation, and finally secured the freedom of the negro. The negro would have been an ingrate, and deserving the contempt of all men, had he not joined his political friends the moment he was set free. The names of Lincoln, Grant, Sumner, Thaddeus Stevens, Chief Justice Chase, Colfax, and those of all the great Republican leaders of the North, were magic names to him. They were associated in his mind with all that was dear to him in freedom, and not to have followed their leadership, would have been an unnatural and ungrateful course of conduct. These men were the heroes that he worshipped, the benefactors to whom he paid homage and reverence, and he followed their lead as naturally as the round-heads followed Cromwell or the French revolutionists Napoleon.

If there had been any hope of the political alliance of the negro with the South, after the war, that hope was dispelled when the whites of the South antagonized all national legislation looking to his enfranchisement and to his elevation to citizenship. They not only opposed it, but with a rancor and violence that were so bitter and inveterate that it took the form of cruelty towards the negro, and proscription and ostracism to the few whites in the South who favored it. The negro would have been less than human had he joined with those he deemed the enemies of his advancement, and cast his vote to defeat his own promotion and amelioration. The Southern whites, who are mostly Democrats, should not judge harshly and unkindly the colored people for this choice of political company. Had they been similarly situated, they would have acted likewise. Such a choice was the only natural and reasonable one.

In this political attitude the Southern negroes have been consistent and persistent. No people ever remained truer to their political convictions and preferences than have they. It is true to-day, as it has been all along, that they are Republicans, and wherever there has been any defection at all, or any apparent departure from their allegiance to this party, it has been temporary and superficial.  At bottom the negro is and has been a Republican.

The solidarity of the whites of the South, in my judgment, has been unfortunate both for the whites and the negroes.  The whites have been associated with the defeated party ever since the war, save during the two terms of Mr. Cleveland's administration.  As a result, the South has received less than its share of the national appropriations, and the millions set apart by Congress for internal improvements have gone for the most part to enrich the East and West.  Had the sectional feeling engendered and kept alive by the attitude of the South, and its virulent and uncompromising animosity toward the Republican party never been, her people would have shared more equally the official favors of the government, and her recuperation from the desolations of war have been instant and rapid.  For these reasons I can but believe that the South has been unwise in her attitude of hostility to the Republican party, which advocated the immediate acceptance of the situation after the war, and progress on the lines of the Thirteenth, Fourteenth and Fifteenth amendments to the Constitution.  The Republican party was composed of the better class of citizens at the North; they were the people of that section who had most of its wealth and intelligence, and who, had they been conciliated and consorted with, instead of the rough and less respectable elements, who constitute the Democratic party of the North, would have been more able to extend help to the poverty-stricken South.

The solidarity of the South likewise has been unfortunate for the colored people. It has been as an impassable and impenetrable wall dividing them from their white neighbors, when they should have been united and harmonious. This political solidarity of the Southern whites has been the cause of the friction which has resulted in most of the strife and bloodshed that has marred the history of the Southern States since the war. Had the negro been in political unity with a large and respectable element of the Southern whites, the bloody annals of Ku Klux times and the disgraceful methods of ballot-box stuffing would not be a part of that history. Political differences have created the chasm between the races, and are responsible, even more than race prejudices, for the deeds of violence committed in the South since the war.

Thus the political alienation of the races in the South has been fraught with evil to both races. A divided house, not on color lines, but on economic lines, would have been a blessing, but when that division has been strictly the outgrowth of

color, and the social and political prejudices incident to that issue, it has been a great evil.

The tendency and drift of things in the South
is now, however, toward the breaking up of old
party associations and affiliations. New issues
are arising, and old political parties are disinte-
grating and realigning themselves. Thousands of
Democrats are beginning to let loose their grip on
the old party they have served so long, and to exercise their individual preferences and convictions
in the matter of suffrage. The great economic
questions and the far-reaching financial issues are
pressing to the front for adjudication and settle-
ment, and the negroes, as well as the whites, are
beginning to see the vital interest they have in
the right solution of these grave matters, and it
may not be many years before the whites and the
negroes will vote side by side in the same political
parties. As yet the negro has shown no disposition to leave his party on national issues. On
merely local and State issues he frequently unites
with his white neighbor, and it is noticeable that
in elections of this kind there is never any suspicion of a false count.

I for one would hail the coming of the day when
the acrimony and partisanship of the past would
be forgotten and buried. I recognize the fact that
the destiny of the negro race is bound up with
that of the Southern whites for the present, if not

for all time. What affects the negro affects the whites. Both alike are interested in good government and clean politics. With the decay of political prejudices and antagonisms, one of the most intricate features of what is called the "negro problem" will be solved. A better feeling would exist, begotten by common political interests, and confidence and peace would reign where distrust and often violence now abound.

Whenever the South will agree that the negro shall deposit his ballot untrammelled and unmolested, then the first step toward political harmony shall have been taken. The whites of the South should not and ought not to expect political peace on such terms. Give the negro his ballot and he will exercise it *for* and not *against* the interests of his own section.

The large vote which was given to Mr. McKinley in the last Presidential election by Southern white people is a straw which indicates the direction the political winds are taking. Thousands more were in sympathy with the issues and principles for which the Republican party stood in that election who never voted at all. This shows that there are forces at work to break up the solidarity of the South, that the party shibboleth can no longer be made the test of patriotism and genuine Southern spirit and the rallying cry of the Southern white masses. It shows that for the future there is a large element at the South who intend to vote their convictions regardless of past party affiliations.

As for the negro, in the division which is inevitably to ensue, he will choose the company of the better class of whites. The populists of the South, representing the least intelligent element of the white people, have failed, and will continue to fail, to enlist the sympathy and co-operation of the negro. It is one characteristic of the negro to like the association of the intelligent and self-respecting classes. Ignorant as he often is, he still refuses to herd with the ignorant and vicious whites, preferring to follow and imitate the better and more enlightened classes. He recognizes the fact that his most powerful and helpful allies are to be found among the strong, conservative and liberal-minded white men of the South, and not with the ignorant, irresponsible and unreliable rabble.

Whatever others may say against Mr. Cleveland, the ex-President, the colored people of this country entertain the highest respect for him as a citizen, a man, and a statesman. He was broad enough to rise above the "color line" and to appoint to responsible positions some worthy colored men. It took some backbone to resist the popular prejudice against such appointments, but he had nerve enough to do so because he thought it was the just and right thing to do. When the history of this country shall be plainly and impartially written, he will occupy a position second only to Andrew Jackson as an uncompromising and unflinching defender of the right as he was permitted to see it.

As to the political future of the colored race I believe that this, like all other questions which are vital to him, will be determined by the factors of religion and education. When by the slow but potent processes of these mighty agencies he shall be qualified for the best and most intelligent citizenship, then he will assert himself with power, and contribute his share in controlling and shaping the legislation of the country. Not only so, but he will add his increment of influence to the industrial, commercial and moral uplift of the whole people, and share in the glory and greatness of Anglo-Saxon progress and civilization.

In the meantime I would appeal to our brother in white to deal with him in the spirit of fairness, throw no obstructions in the way of his suffrage, convince him that you are his friend and not his foe, let him exercise the right of life, liberty and property as the Constitution directs, and then he will not distrust but confide in you as his ally and brother. He has no desire to injure the white man, he does not wish to abridge the rights and privileges of his white neighbor. All he asks is that you give him equal rights before the law, treat him as a citizen and a freeman, and in turn he will love and trust you, stand shoulder to shoulder with you, and join you in the march to national greatness and honor.

# CHAPTER XX.

## THE HOME-LIFE OF THE NEGRO.

IN the years of slavery the negro dwelt usually in a cabin made of logs. These cabins were generally close together in the plantation-yard· They were rude in construction, but as the climate was mild and fire-wood plentiful, there was very little suffering from cold.

It was impossible in such homes to cultivate the domestic side of life—to develop the home-loving and home-adorning spirit. A plain wooden table, a rude bed and a few benches, and sometimes plain split-bottomed chairs, were the articles of furniture usually found in the cabin of the Southern slave.

But since the advent of freedom, and the general improvement in the intelligence of the colored people, consequent thereupon, their home-life has been greatly bettered, and among the more intelligent and thrifty of the race may be found homes exhibiting every evidence of refinement and neatness and comfort. There are, of course, different degrees of refinement among the well-to-do colored people just as there is among the whites. For, after all, the qualities of elegance and neatness reside more in individuals than they do in races.

The home-life of the well-to-do Southern negro is improving every day. Music, which is an art the negro naturally acquires, is a characteristic feature in his home. The natural melody of his voice has been admitted on all hands, and in thousands of homes culture is giving to his songs a bewitching sweetness which is charming and beautiful. He is beginning to learn the use of better instruments than the Jewsharp and the banjo. The men and women quickly learn to play upon the guitar and the mandolin, and even the piano. Music has always played its part in the civilizing and humanizing of men. Among the Greeks it was cultivated as an art with the same assiduity as painting, sculpture and architecture. Orpheus lives in Greek mythology, and Apollo, with his lute, held high place among the honored divinities. Hebrew melody is immortal in the songs of Miriam and Deborah and the psalms of David and Asaph. The negro, through music, is taking into his home-life the softening, refining and uplifting power of melody. Sacred music he especially cultivates, and the beautiful and weird songs one may hear in almost any congregation of colored people give to their worship a peculiar and powerful impressiveness.

The more intelligent of the negroes are beginning, too, to recognize the influence of art as a factor in the improvement of their homes. They are beginning to understand its educative effect, its refining and elevating tendency. No less than music, art has its office in the civilization of a race. The paintings of Raphael, Murillo, Titan and Sir Joshua Reynolds have accomplished almost as much for men as literature, and wherever we see art stressed in the home we may be sure that refinement of some sort characterizes its inmates. I am, by reason of my official relation to my church, thrown constantly into the homes of the well-to-do of my race. I have been astonished and gratified by the exhibition of pictures, bric-a-brac and ornamentations of various kinds which adorn these homes. This shows that the minds of the better informed of my race have passed out of the stage of the semi-barbarism in which emancipation found them, and are opening to the susceptibilities of civilized life. At the Exposition held in Atlanta, Ga., in 1895, the building, devoted to the exhibition of the handiwork of the negro, contained many beautiful specimens of paintings and hundreds of articles made by their hands, which showed wonderful artistic proficiency. This was considered marvellous when it was remembered that only thirty years of freedom have been theirs.

Another hopeful sign in the home life of the ne-

gro is seen in the number of libraries these homes
contain. Since they have learned to read, many
of them are accumulating well-selected books.
Good books, next to association with the pure and
cultured, are the most potent of all civilizing
agencies. The Bible, the book of books, is in
every well-to-do home in the South, and, with it,
choice specimens of literature both religious and
secular. The young generation are being taught
to read these choice productions of the learned
and pious, and are slowly but surely imbibing high
thoughts and noble aspirations from them. It has
been said that if you can get people to read, you
can safely predict their civilization. But never
until books are placed in the homes of the people
will they become a reading people. Our people
have made a gratifying start in this direction.
The leading men of our race need to stress more
and more the necessity of home libraries, which
will furnish the opportunity for knowledge to our
people they so much need. They should assist,
too, in judiciously selecting for the families with
whom they are acquainted, the books that are to
occupy a place upon the shelves of these home
libraries.

We find further in the home life of our intelligent colored people, a family-loving sentiment.
The negro mother and father, if they have had
any training at all, love their children. The

brutal treatment of their offspring, which, we are free to admit, has been common in the South, is confined, for the most part, to the ignorant and the vicious members of my race.  I have been in thousands of homes where the amenities and urbanities of life were practiced by the different members of the family with uniform and beautiful consistency.  I have known colored mothers to make every sacrifice to educate their children, and colored fathers to toil until they were worn out to feed and clothe them.  It is a slander upon the negro race to charge them with a want of proper affection for their children.  This is true only of the most ignorant and immoral of them.  And this is true also of the ignorant and vicious of every race.  No home life, among any people, is more mixed with the "milk of human kindness," more characterized by the virtues of forbearance, gentleness and politeness than the homes of the better class of Southern negroes.

They are attentive to their sick and show often to the afflicted in their households a tender consideration that is admirable and beautiful.  No more gentle, soothing, sympathizing nurses can be found in the world than the best type of our colored women.  It may be that often, through ignorance, they fail to use the proper hygienic means for the health of their children, but it is a rare case where the children of intelligent colored parents suffer for the lack of devoted attention. Another thing that illustrates the natural kindness of the negro race is the care which they take of the children of their deceased kinspeople. Almost every colored family has in it orphan children. I have known many of them to take the children of their dead sisters and brothers, more of them than they had of their own, and rear them with the same care as if they had been their own children. Perhaps this is one reason why there is so little pauperism among them. There are fewer beggars and tramps among this race than perhaps among any other, except it be the Jews.

The negro is naturally mirthful. Though his home be humble, he brightens it with laughter and good cheer. Their happy voices make the log cabins of the South resound with merriment, and often with boisterous hilarity. They are not given to the moody reverie, the quiet, tranquil existence characteristic of the whites. They love to talk and to jest, to dance and to sing, to frolic and to play, and it is the rarest sight imaginable to see them with sad countenances. Though their fare be scanty and their garments worn and threadbare, they are as well contented as the rich in their palaces of splendor and plenty. Hence their home life, as a rule, is bright and cheery. No people ever bore up under such hardships with equal contentment and resignation. The Israelites

murmured against God in the midst of the weariness and woes of the wilderness.   Not so the
negro.   With happy heart he thanks his Maker
for all that comes and goes, smiling through poverty and oppression to whatever lot his destiny
may appoint.

In their home life the more intelligent of my
race are beginning to pay attention to the culinary
art, and to vary their diet both as to the food
itself and the manner of preparing it.   In former
times they cooked their bread, made of Indian
corn, in the ashes, and fried their bacon in a skillet.   But they are gradually laying aside the
skillet and the ash-bed for the cooking-stove and
the range, and the colored housewives are becoming experts in the culinary art.   Nothing of a material nature is more civilizing than proper diet,
properly served.   It is around the well-prepared
board that a people learn the manners of civilized
life, and get the food which is necessary to supply
the brain with thought-making power.   I rejoice
to see such marked advance among my people in
this regard, and see in it one of the signs of real
improvement in their material and social condition.

As to the social life of the negroes it may be
said that it has not yet taken definite shape.   In
the country districts there is no caste.   They are
on terms of equality and mingle indiscriminately.
But there is beginning to assert itself a decided

disposition to ostracize from the better element of negroes those who are grossly lacking in virtue and decency. Our people have been too loose in their social relations; they have not sufficiently emphasized their condemnation of vice and impurity by relegating to the rear that class who are flagrantly vicious and impure. I recognize the fact that we need to create a stronger sentiment against vice by refusing to tolerate in our best social life those who are unworthy and corrupt. There is a very observable tendency among what are called the mulattoes to withdraw themselves from the dark-skinned negroes and set up for themselves a distinct social class. This has its bearing upon the home life of our race, often determining the matter of hospitality and marriage. It is dividing the negroes as nothing else does, and is threatening, helped as it is by constant miscegenation with the white race, to obliterate the dark-skinned negro.

# CHAPTER XXI.

## THE RELIGION OF THE NEGRO.

IT has been said that man is a religious animal. It is pre-eminently true of the negro. Whatever may be the personal character of an individual of this race, he never questions the existence of a Supreme Being, or doubts the existence of a future state of rewards and punishment.

His religion may be defective in its practical relation to the principles of right conduct and living, but it is always sound as to the faith which it inspires in God and revelation. Infidelity has never taken any hold on my people. In almost every community there is a church building, rude though some of them may be, where they assemble to worship God. An atheist or an infidel is a rare specimen, and excites as much curiosity as a bear escaped from some traveling menagerie.

The worship of the negro is one of the simplest sort. He has no appreciation of elaborate rituals, of services consisting of forms and ceremonies. Hence, the great mass of the colored race have united either with the Methodist or Baptist Churches. These churches have the simplest,

185

least complicated forms of church service, and the
negro naturally gravitates to them.

The emotional nature is highly developed in
the negro. He is easily and powerfully impressed
by all that appeals to his sympathies and affections. This accounts for the fact that there are
so many natural orators among them. Perhaps
no race has developed so many eloquent speakers
as the colored people of the South have produced
in the last thirty years. For the most part the
talent of the negro has sought the pulpit for its
expression, and many wonderfully eloquent men
have adorned the pulpits of the Methodist and
Baptist churches in the South. These great leaders, under God, have built up two of the most
wonderful branches of the Christian Church in all
this land of ours.

Speaking as a representative of my own church,
the African Methodist Episcopal Church, and
viewing the question from the standpoint of my
own experience and observation, I would say that
the admirable characteristics of the religion of the
negro are :

First. Its simple unquestioning faith. Indeed,
the faith element is so strong that often, when not
intelligently directed, it runs into superstition. I
have never known of but one trial for heresy
among the ministry or the laity of my church.
They receive, with absolute trust, the doctrines of

the Bible as formulated by the churches to which
they adhere, and though in practice they are often
lax and flagrantly immoral, in their theory of religion, they are orthodox and sound. This faith
is not the outcome of ignorance alone, as many
have sneeringly suggested. There are many scholarly men and women among us in the schools and
the pulpit who manifest the same simple and
child-like faith. The truth is, the faith faculty is
strong in the negro, and religion is a necessity of his
nature.

Another characteristic of the religion of the
negro is its fervency. I have already spoken of
the strength of his emotional nature, but its mani-
festation in his religious life gives it its most distinctive expression. He loves the moving, stirring
appeal, and revels in the full tide of emotional
feeling. He has no toleration for the coldly intellectual discourse, and the quiet, formal worship.
He likes to be moved to tears, to be touched
deeply in his emotions, to be swept off his feet by
the thrilling, the pathetic, the awe-inspiring. It
is often true, no doubt, that in this unrestrained
vent of feeling he swings to the extreme, and
sometimes mistakes mere physical excitement for
divine unction ; but it were better for him to err in
this direction, than to choose a cold, icy, formal
mode of worship, which so deadens all religious life
and delight, as to destroy its power over him and his

pleasure in it. Of the two extremes—dead formalism and a mere religious emotionalism—I should prefer the latter, worthless though both may be. But mere physical emotion is not the whole of the negro's religion. Beneath his deep feelings there are often a spiritual and a divine energy and power, which take hold upon the heart and life, and give them uplift and inspiration and purity. I, for one, am proud of the emotional warmth and susceptibility of my people. I like to see it in the beaming faces, to hear it in the transporting, thrilling songs, to feel it in the fervent, hearty hand-shake of my race. So long as the negro is true to his native endowment and temperament he will ever evince emotion in his religious worship.

Another marked characteristic of the religion of the negro is its benevolence. I do not believe any people have ever given as much, with so little of wealth to give from, as the colored people of America. It is marvelous what they have given for the erection of church edifices and the support of their church institutions since they were made free thirty-two years ago. If written out, it would make a chapter of self-sacrifice and heroism without a parallel in the history of mankind. From their small earnings they set apart a certain sum, and this is given Sabbath after Sabbath with a regularity that is as beautiful as it is constant.

When men give to a cause, and keep giving with a devotion that never tires, they at least show their love for that cause and the value they put upon it. Judged by this rule, the negro puts the highest estimate upon his religion and cherishes it as he does nothing else in this world. This benevolence takes many directions. Christian negroes are proverbially hospitable. They will share their last crust of bread with their needy and helpless brethren. They open their hearts and homes for the entertainment of Christian workers and ministers, feeling it a proud privilege to have in their houses the servants of the Lord. The negro has no element of selfishness nor *stinginess* in his nature, and his record of charity and benevolent giving proves it without question.

The African Methodist Church alone contributed for all purposes during last year, 1896, nearly two millions of dollars. And other colored churches have shown like liberality. Indeed, it is one of the marvelous facts of this age that the negro, out of his poverty, has given so much to the cause which is nearest of all to his heart.

I am not so blind as not to see that the religion of the negroes needs improvement. Many reproaches are justly laid at our door, and we should not deny or indignantly resent them, but enlist all our consecrated powers to rectify and remove them.

And the first of these stigmas which attaches to our various colored churches is the impurity of some of our ministers. I say our ministers because I am better acquainted with the moral status of our preachers than I am with that of the ministers of other denominations. I do not believe that we are more lax than the ministry of other churches. I will say farther that I believe that only a small per cent. of the ministry of any of our evangelical churches are impure.

The church of God must find her exponents in the representative men who stand up before the world as the guardians of her doctrines and the exemplars of her teachings. If the church suffers through the lapses and inconsistencies of her private membership, how much more must she receive reproach through the derelictions and immoralities of her ministry? "Like priest like people," is as true to-day as it was in the time of the prophet. The anathemas of the Saviour were hurled at the wicked priests whose vices were a standing menace to the purity of the Jewish Church, and who stood in the way of the conversion and salvation of the common people.

It is as true to-day as it was then that an impure ministry is the greatest obstacle to the growth and the power of the church. Let men venerate the character and life of the watchmen who stand upon the walls of Zion, and they will respect and venerate the church, and bow to the authority with which she is vested. Let them behold an unworthy ministry—inconsistent in life and practice—and they will withhold their respect for the church and their allegiance to her institutions.

I maintain that the utmost caution should be observed in the selection and ordination of men to discharge these sacred functions. The doors of the ministry should be barred against men of doubtful record and shady antecedents. They injure both them and the church when they are allowed a place among the worthy and deserving ministers of the church. I need not appeal to the worthy and consecrated ministers of all our colored churches, of which, thank God, there are many to endorse these views. All true ministers of the gospel are interested profoundly in a clean ministry. They find themselves hampered and discounted in their own work by the bad odor of other ministers. Let them see to it that " wolves in sheep's clothing" are kept out of the fold.

Again, we need to remove the reproach which is often brought against us of a lack of deep pity. There can be no question of the soundness of the negro's faith. It is only in the matter of his practice, his conformity to his creed, that criticism can find any just basis when applied to his religious life. In any judgment of the negro in this regard, it should be remembered for sweet charity's sake, that only forty-three per cent. of them can read and write, and that the class who constitute this forty-three per cent. belong to those who have been born since the war. It could not be expected of a race which, until recently, could show but a small percentage of intelligence, that they should manifest a high degree of moral and religious excellence. I confess that it has been marvelous to me that my people under such limitations and disadvantages should have shown such a response to the demands of a high and worthy Christian life. And in this respect I believe, from a wide observation on this line, that there is a steady progress—a constant improvement. Yet there is much to lament in the looseness of our morals as professing Christians. "Faith is dead without works," and until we show forth the beauty of religion in our lives, our profession will be vain. Would to God that we could boast purity in all our women, integrity and honesty in all our men, a high type of genuine, scriptural piety in all our churches. Then indeed would our Zion be beautiful to behold, "fair as the moon and terrible as an army with banners." This with us, as with all churches of every race, should be the ideal to which we should constantly look and work. With more enlightenment and better knowledge of the Bible, I believe that the type of religion among my people will be constantly made

better, and as time goes on we will lift from our
Zion the shadow of reproach, and in the personal
and individual character of our membership present to the world the best ideals of Christian
living.

Finally, we need more unanimity of spirit in
our religious life. There is too much of disunion
and disharmony among us. In many instances it
is the outgrowth of a spirit of ambition, a desire
to be "chief" instead of to be the "servant or
all." Most of the troubles we have had in our
churches has been the result of this spirit. Fac-
tional disturbances have often marred the peace of
Zion, and our strength been wasted by these un-
seemly divisions. The combative spirit in the
negro shows itself perhaps more prominently in
these church disputes than anywhere else. These
things ought not so to be.

# CHAPTER XXII.

## RIGHT TREATMENT URGED.

IN what I shall write on the subject of the relation of the two races, I shall occupy the standpoint of the colored man. Of course it is to be expected that a negro will view this question differently from the white man. His condition and circumstances, his peculiar racial differentiation from the Caucasian, his past history as a slave, give to the whole question of his relation to the white man in this country a deep and absorbing interest. Many have discussed this question, various and divergent views have been presented, and yet the problem has not been fully solved. Nothing I shall say will be inspired by a feeling of unkindness or ill will, and with no purpose to create strife or division. For my white brother I have nothing but love and good will. Neither will I attempt to magnify unduly the virtues and strong qualities of my own people. I wish to be as fair, impartial and just as it is possible for one to be.

And first I can say that there is not, so far as I know, anything like prejudice or hatred toward the white man on the part of the negro, because he is white. He does not cherish mere race animosity. There can be no doubt but that the whites do cherish this race prejudice. They regard the negro with a feeling of inferiority, and look with something of contempt upon him as a race. The negro has nothing of this feeling. He looks with admiration upon the wonderful civilization the white man has wrought and strives constantly to imitate and to emulate him.

The negro no longer cherishes unkind feelings toward the Southern whites on account of the institution of slavery. The responsibility for the introduction of slavery in this country must be put where it belongs, upon those who have long since passed away. Most of the old slave-holders, too, have died, and a new generation of whites have come to the fore. For the wrongs the negro has suffered there must ever be sorrow and regret. It is indeed a dark and unsightly page on the book of the world's history. But it would be unfair to charge slavery or its wrongs to the present generation of Southern whites. And I do not believe that the negro, as a race, has any feeling of resentment on account of these things toward their white neighbors. They have forgiven the wrongs of the past, and are striving to forget them in their march to better things.

It is not of the past that the negro complains; it is of the present. Kind, just, cordial, brotherly treatment *now*, would wipe out all bitter remembrances and bring the negro to love and honor the white man more and more. What the negro desires is that the white man should meet him on the broad platform of a common brotherhood and give him a fair chance in the race of life.

The foreigner, born in distant lands, an alien, and often an enemy to American institutions, is welcomed to American shores. He is given instant recognition and sometimes distinguished consideration. He is admitted to the competitions of American life and given free entrance into all avenues and departments of industrial life. Not so is the poor negro treated. Ostracism is for the most part his lot, his contact is shunned, except in the capacity of a menial, as if his presence were pollution. On the cars, in places of amusement, at public gatherings of all sorts, his contact is deemed disreputable, and his presence an affront.

Personally I make no complaint. Holding a high office in my church, I am given kind and distinguished consideration where this fact is known, and I fully appreciate the courteous and polite attentions I receive. But I am speaking for my people, and I can but see the disposition of the white people to hold off from their colored neighbor as if he did not belong to the same human family.

Be it understood that I am not pleading for social equality. No man understands better than

I do that the social life of a people cannot be regulated and controlled by legislation. This must be determined by the laws of affinity, the principles of individual preference and choice over which government has no power and which legislative enactments cannot create nor destroy. I would be as far from entering a home or from thrusting myself into merely social relations when my presence was not wanted as any man living. It is unnatural for any man or set of men to wish to identify themselves with the purely social relations of others when their presence is regarded with disfavor. It is not, then, because his brother in white refuses to recognize his social equality in these particulars that the negro complains.

To be candid, it is this that he objects to; he does not think he is treated with fairness when he is looked down upon as inferior on account of his color, if he is deserving of regard and consideration in other respects; that he should always be deemed as one of God's creatures to be tolerated, but not recognized as a brother man; to be permitted a seat in a railway car as a nurse, but not as a citizen; to be allowed to sweep the floor of a hall of public amusement, but not as a listener to be entertained. This distinction between the colored servant, nurse and the colored floor-sweeper, and the colored citizen, seems to be putting a premium on merely menial service, and disparaging any honorable ambition a colored man may have to rise above the sphere of a nurse or a body-servant. In other words, the legislation of some Southern States, and the practice of many Southern whites, is directed against the commendable aspirations of the colored race. He is really forbidden to aspire to be a self-respecting citizen. "You cannot enter here." "Seat thou thyself there." "You are a negro, therefore be forever a menial, and sit thou forever in the back seat." This is the interpretation of the conduct of his white brother toward him in the South and in some sections of the North.

In reply, our white brother says: "Yes, this is true, but it is the penalty the negro must pay for his color." This, then, is the chasm that divides the races. There will be no dispute as to this. The white man admits it. The colored man feels the sting of it. Could some ingenious pharmacist prepare a compound that would change the color of the negro's skin to the color of the Caucasian, the race problem would be solved, and the last barrier removed that divides the races. Alas, for the colored man, no such a compound can be found, short of infusion, through the process of amalgamation.

But is this difference in color sufficient to create a line of separation over which the negro is never to pass? Did God, who of one blood made all men, intend the color to keep in eternal antagonism the two races, which are equally the offspring of his own creative power and love?

I am free to admit that the negro has helped to create a sentiment against his own color. He has accepted the stigma which the white man has put upon his dark skin and acquiesced in the estimate which he has been pleased to put upon African blood. This he has done without such protest as he should have made against the injustice of that stigma. The Indian is proud that he is a red man; the Chinaman is proud that he is a yellow man; the Anglo-Saxon is proud that he is a white man. Why should not the negro be proud that he is a black man? Is there any element of inferiority in the dark color, which is his?

The reason why the negro does not take pride in his color is because it has been made the sign of his degradation, the symbol and the evidence of his inferiority by the white man. His treatment, by reason of his color, has taught him to dislike his color, and to attribute all his injuries and slights to that cause. If he is ostracised, it is because he has a dark skin; if he is elbowed out of the better and more lucrative places of business, if he is remanded to the rear in all competitive struggles in the work and walk of life, it is because the Almighty did not see fit to give his skin the same color as that of his Anglo-Saxon brother.

Hence, it is generally the case, the negro is glad of the white infusion of blood he has received through miscegenation. He finds that the lighter his skin is, the more he is admired by his own race and the more he is preferred by the white race. In many instances the mixture of white with negro blood is a matter of pride and boasting with those so amalgamated, and has created a social class called mulattoes. These separate themselves from the negroes of darker skins, and affect a feeling of superiority. The negro has thus been educated to look upon his color as a mark of degradation. The white man has taught him so to regard it, and he has too willingly fallen in with his teaching. This estimate of color the negro should be taught is purely the result of that prejudice which originated in and was perpetuated by slavery. He should be taught that his color is his inheritance from God, and that no degradation attaches to it. He should be taught that intelligence, honesty, uprightness constitute the nobility of individuals and races, and these will make him worthy of respect and honor, no matter what his color may be.

The white man bases his aversion to association with the negro upon the ground that he is not a cognate race. But the only evidence of this fact is the color of his skin at last. He holds that the obliteration of the "color line" will be the first step to complete amalgamation. Practically, however, the color line is ignored, and miscegenation goes on hourly. One million and upwards of mulattoes tell the story, besides as many more with a slight admixture of Caucasian blood. The law forbids intermarriage and curtails the social and civil rights of the negroes in the South, but it is powerless to reach the great tide of miscegenation which threatens at length to wipe out the color line despite the prejudices and the legislation against it. If the American negro be not a cognate race in the next hundred years, it will not be the fault of the Southern whites who, through the process of unlawful amalgamation, are so rapidly infusing in his veins the Caucasian blood.

Be it understood that I am not contending for what is known as "social equality," a legalized equality which forces association of whites with whites, or of whites with negroes. As I have stated, this question must be left to natural laws which grow out of personal and social affinities. I am now contending only for that social equality which is designated as civil rights. I believe with all my heart that a colored man, if he pays for it, is entitled to as good a seat in a railway car as any other man. So long as he is driven from decent places and decent surroundings as an object of detestation, so long will he be taught to yield his own self respect, and so long will the white race look down upon him as a menial, a groundling and a slave.

Such treatment of the negro as will teach him to respect himself will not bring about the friction and trouble the white people of the South anticipate. Only the better class of colored people, those who are neat in person and well-to-do in purse, as a general thing, would be able to claim first-class accommodations. In the street cars of all our Southern cities, colored people ride with white people. This does not create friction, and here, owing to the cheapness of fare, the least respectable colored classes are admitted to seats side by side with white people. This shows that the separation of the races in the railway car, and at places of amusement, and at public gatherings, generally, is the outgrowth of a prejudice which has made such separation a custom, and that it is not founded in reason or common sense.

I would impress this thought upon my brothers in white: Do not always be flaunting in the negro's face the " red flag" of color. Do not drive him like a hunted beast from all places of respectability. If he is a gentleman in appearance and intelligence, do not seek to degrade him by pushing him aside. If he is able to pay his way, let him get the benefit of his money, and whenever he violates the laws of propriety and good breeding, call him down just as you would an ill-bred and an ill-mannered white man.

# CHAPTER XXIII.

## SHALL THE NEGRO EMIGRATE?

THE question of emigration is not a new one. It has been discussed and experimented with since emancipation. Colonization has been favored by men of wise heads and who possessed a thorough knowledge of the peculiar circumstances of the colored people in this country. These have maintained that it is the only safe and speedy solution of the negro problem. That they were honest in their advocacy of colonization none will question. Every scheme to this end, however, has not only failed, but failed signally and completely, and there is not a single encouragement furnished by any past experiment for any plan of colonization.

I have systematically and conscientiously opposed emigration whenever I have had occasion to consider the subject. I have never seen any prospect for the betterment of my race in any scheme of colonization that has ever been suggested. I have always believed that America is the best place for the American negro, and that here he can and will work out the highest destiny possible for him. I have accepted what I believe to be the purpose of Providence in permitting his location here and in keeping him here to fulfill the highest ends that Providence has in view for him.

It can but be apparent to him who seriously considers the subject that it would be a foolish thing, if it were feasible, for the negro at this period of his history, to relinquish the civilization that surrounds him and go out to the wilds of some unpeopled wilderness which has not been touched by the light of modern thought and ideas —to leave the contact of the inspiring and elevating forces which environ him, and dump himself down to the vast solitudes of Africa or any other country. It would in some respects be like the conduct of the prodigal, who left his splendid home to herd with the swine and to feed upon the husks.

I have not opposed the emigration of individuals, men of our race with means, or men with special gifts for missionary work among the untutored and the uncivilized. Let them go if they desire, or if they feel moved by the Spirit of God, and my best wishes and my prayers will go with them. But for the negroes of this country, as a race, to undertake to emigrate to Africa, or any other foreign country, I have thought, and still think, would be a suicidal step fraught with blight and ruin to the interests and the hopes of my people.

Such a scheme, in the first place, is thoroughly

impracticable in any view of it, for to be worth anything it must be accomplished in a short time. Slow emigration would result in the loss of all the negro has gained, for the few would be absorbed into the many. To be a successful scheme of emigration it must be an exodus like that of the Israelites, when the whole nation went at once, and not a hoof nor a horn was left behind. Even with all the multitudes of Israel bound by a common suffering and a common deliverance, it was almost impossible to preserve them from the idolatry of the Caananites. The slow emigration of the American negro to Africa, or any other new foreign country, would mean his disintegration as a race and his absorption into foreign and heathen fetichism.

But the scheme of immediate colonization as a race is utterly impracticable. If it be to Africa, the only country that offers any physical advantages for the planting of so large a colony, the cost of transporting a race of eight millions of people would be an insuperable difficulty. Who would furnish the money, who would fit out the ships, who would support the race until it became self-supporting, and no man can compute how long this would be. Lands would have to be cleared, houses built, and all the necessary appurtenances and improvements gotten together for the pursuit of agriculture, the only occupation the

negro as a race is acquainted with. Then there is
the danger of a new climate, which at first would
bring on new and numerous diseases. The negro
has already passed through the ordeal of violent
climatic changes when he was brought to America,
and fifty per cent. of them died in their removal
from Africa to Jamaica and the West India
Islands. He would have to repeat the same experience in his return to Africa. None but an
enthusiast and a dreamer would advocate sudden
and wholesale emigration.

Emigration is not only impracticable, but unde-
sirable. It is better to remain where we are, even
if it were practicable to go away. Here we have
schools in operation of every grade, from the public school to the university. Millions have been
invested in plants for our education. Colleges,
normal institutes, seminaries, high schools, are
here to fit our young men and women for intelligent, cultured citizenship. Our people too are
rapidly becoming land-owners; they are investing
in town and city property, as we have shown else-
where, and multitudes of them own good, com-
fortable homes. The colored man is practically
in possession of the best lands in the South as ten-
ants. To leave all these advantages and go forth
into an unknown country under new conditions,
it seems to me would be madness.

Contact with Anglo-Saxon civilization is no

small advantage the negro would have to surrender in any scheme of colonization. In his present formative state he needs this environment. He touches now every day the greatest race that has yet appeared on the earth, the race whose genius and valor have conquered upon every field, and left every other nation and people far to the rear in their splendid march to conquest and power. The negro has the imitative faculty to a high degree, and quickly and readily absorbs what he sees and hears. Here he is beginning to take on a good degree of civilization. He is becoming an architect and a builder, a merchant, a teacher, a minister, and a scientific agriculturist. He is entering slowly the learned professions as opportunity will allow, and becoming a lawyer, a physician, an engineer, and is filling other places requiring skill, and training, and culture. It seems to me that at present he is in the best possible environment for him, and to leave it upon a venture would be the sum of folly, the worst possible step he could take.

Again, the negro has become attached to the land of his adoption. Here he has suffered, it is true, but here, too, he has rejoiced. Here he was born, here his ancestors for generations were born. Here he first saw the sun of liberty rise, and here he heard first the bugle notes of freedom which fell like music on his soul. It is his labor that has largely created the wealth of the South, that has cut down the native forests, dug out of her soil untold wealth, and enriched her fair domain. Here sleep the ashes of his loved ones, and sacred memories gather about all the hills and valleys of this his adopted yet native home. The negro loves America. The Stars and the Stripes is the symbol to him of his liberty, and next to God it is the holiest object to his heart. Here he wishes to live, to identify himself with American history and glory, and share in the brightening destiny of American institutions. He does not wish to be torn from these associations and environments. Deep down in his heart is an abiding patriotism. It is this that makes America the most revered of all countries. He has learned to call it "my country," and to defend it against every foe, he would gladly give his life. A few now and then have gone back to Africa, but the great masses have been deaf to all emigration appeals, because they loved the South and America too well to leave. So long as this love abides in his heart, so long will he keep his present domicile.

It is urged by those who have persistently advocated emigration that the negro ought to go, because his presence is not desired here by his white neighbor and brother. So far from this being so, the very opposite seems the case. Emigration has had, perhaps, its greatest foe in the white man. He opposed it bitterly from the beginning. The white people of the South recognize the fact that the negro makes the best laborer in the world, and that, as a citizen, he is preferable in every way to the foreigner, no matter from what country he may come. It is a mistake to say that any considerable number of the citizens of the South desire now, or ever have desired, the emigration of the negro. On the contrary, they have thrown every obstacle in the way to prevent it. In many States the legislatures have imposed heavy fines upon emigration agents, whose purpose was simply to remove them from State to State. The imputation, then, that the negro is remaining in the South against the wishes of the South, is gratuitous and grossly contrary to the truth. If there is any charge to make, it is that the white people have too bitterly opposed even the smallest movement looking to emigration by the negro. I will admit that a few individuals, including Senator Morgan, of Alabama, have advocated emigration, but the great masses of the Southern people have persistently and bitterly fought it at every step.

The friends of emigration, among the leading colored people of America, have based their appeal further upon the unfair and unjust treatment the negro receives at the hands of the Southern whites. This is the only argument that has been advanced for emigration, as it appears to me, that has any real force in it. Whenever it shall appear that it is the fixed purpose and policy of the whites to withhold justice from the negro, to refuse him protection before the law in all just demands, to look with favor upon lawless mobs who, without pretext of law, take him by force from his home or from the custody of the officers of the law and violently assault him and sometimes cruelly murder him for alleged but unproven crimes, then it will be time for the negro to accept whatever scheme of emigration that may be offered to leave the home and country of his adoption. To remain longer, under such cruel conditions, would not only be fatal to his happiness and contentment, but a crime committed against himself and his children, which no aspiring and self-respecting people would consent to.

I do not believe that such a juncture in the history of the Southern negro has yet been reached. I believe that it is the design and purpose of the legally-constituted authorities in the South, and of the large body of the intelligent and law-abiding white people of that section, to deal fairly with the negroes, at least in the matter of life, liberty and property. And I affirm that this class looks with disfavor and reprehension upon lawless methods and procedures in dealing with their colored neighbors. Still, with all this,

the colored man is often the victim of injustice
and cruelty. Race prejudice often operates to
defeat justice before the courts, and to rob him of
the hard-earned rewards of toil. We hope and
believe that a righteous sentiment, demanding
and requiring kind treatment, honest dealing and
strict justice towards the negro, will permeate the
entire masses of Southern whites, and that the
day is not far distant when lawlessness, mob-rule
and cruelty will be things of the past.

Emigration for the negro is growing less and
less popular among the negroes themselves. They
have been fleeced time and again by so-called emigration agents, tramps and frauds, who have prac-
tised upon their credulity to swindle and defraud
them. They have come at length to see, those of
them who have looked with some degree of favor
upon colonization, that it is a dream and a delusion, and with a practical unanimity the race has
settled the question, and have made up their
minds to work out the problem of their destiny in
the South and Southwest, where they are at
present located. That they are wise in this decision, no man who looks candidly and dispassion-
ately at the situation can have a reasonable doubt.
Time will cure many of the ills under which we
suffer to-day. Growing intelligence and improving financial conditions will dispose of many
questions, which now seem perplexing and insolv-

able. Broader and more Christian views, on the part of the whites, will dispel much of the prejudice and injustice which now exist, and the negro will march on to his destiny in the South with the good-will of his white brother and with the smiles of Almighty God upon him.

# CHAPTER XXIV.

## AN APPEAL TO OUR BROTHER IN WHITE.

PROVIDENCE, in wisdom, has decreed that the lot of the negro should be cast with the white people of America. Condemn as we may the means through which we were brought here, recount as we may the suffering through which, as a race, we passed in the years of slavery, yet the fact remains that to-day our condition is far in advance of that of the negroes who have never left their native Africa. We are planted in the midst of the highest civilization mankind has ever known, and are rapidly advancing in knowledge, property and moral enlightenment. We might, with all reason, thank God even for slavery, if this were the only means through which we could arrive at our present progress and development.

We should indeed account ourselves blest if our white brethren would always extend to us that kindness, justice and sympathy which our services to them in the past should inspire, and our dependence upon them as the more enlightened and wealthy race should prompt them to bestow.

Why should there be prejudice and dislike on the part of the white man to his colored brother?

Is it because he was once a slave, and a slave must forever wear the marks of degradation? Is there no effacement for the stigma of slavery—no erasement for this blot of shame? Will our white brother not remember that it was his hand that forged the links of that chain and that riveted them around the necks of a people that had roved for thousands of years in the unrestrained liberty of their boundless forests in far-away Africa? As well might the seducer blacken the name and reputation of the fair and spotless maiden he had cruelly and wantonly seduced. Go far enough back and it is more than probable that you will find the taint of slavery in your line and its blot upon your escutcheon. The proud Saxon became the slave to the Norman, and yet to-day millions are proud to be called Anglo-Saxons.

Will our white brother refuse us his cordial fellowship because of our ignorance? Ignorance is indeed a great evil and hinderance. The enlightened and refined cannot fellowship the ignorant the benighted, the untutored. If this be the line of demarkation, we can and will remove it. No people ever made more heroic efforts to rise from ignorance to enlightenment. Forty-three per cent. of the negro race can read and write, and with time we can bring our race up to a high degree of civilization. We are determined, by the help of Providence, and the strength of our own right

arms, to educate our people until the reproach of
ignorance can no longer be brought against us.
When we do, will our white brothers accord that
respect which is due intelligence and culture?

Does our white brother look with disdain upon
us because we are not cleanly and neat? It is
true that the masses of our race have not shown that
regard for personal cleanliness and nicety of dress,
which a wealthy and educated people have the
means and the time to do. Our people, by the
exigencies of their lot, have had to toil and toil in
the menial places, the places where drudgery was
demanded and where contact with dust and filth
was necessary to the accomplishment of their work.
But even this can be remedied, and cleanliness and
neatness can be made a part of the negro's education until they can present, as thousands of them
are now doing, a creditable appearance. Will improvement along these lines help us to gain the
esteem and respectful consideration of our white
brothers? If so, the time is not far distant when
this barrier will be removed. Education will help
solve this difficulty as it does all others, and give
to our race that touch of refinement which insures
physical as well as mental soundness—*sano mens
in sano corpora.*

But is our moral condition the true reason of our
ostracism? Are we remanded to the back seats
and ever held in social dishonor because we are

morally unclean?  Would that we could reply by
a denial of the allegation, and rightly claim that
purity which should be at the foundation of all
respectable social life.  But here we ask the charitable judgment of our white brethren, and point
them to the heroic efforts we have made and are
making for the moral elevation of our race.  Even
a superficial glance at the social side of the negro's
life will convince the unprejudiced that progress is
being made among the better classes of our people
toward virtuous living.  Chastity is being urged
everywhere in the school-house, and the church,
and the home, for our women, and honesty and
integrity for our men.  We can and will lift the
shadow of immorality from the great masses of our
race, and demonstrate to the whole world what religion and education can do for a people.  We are
doing it.  Among the thoroughly cultured and
rightly trained of our women, virtue is as sacred
as life, and among our young men of similar advantages, honor and integrity are prized as highly
as among any people on the globe.

Is our poverty the barrier that divides us from
a closer fellowship with our white brethren?
Would wealth cure all the evils of our condition,
and give us the cordial recognition we ask from
them?  If so, we can remove even this barrier.
Our labor has already created much of the wealth
of the South, and it only needs intelligence to

turn it into our own coffers and make it the possession of our own people. Among the whites
money seems to be the *sesame* that opens the doors
to social recognition, and converts the veriest
shoddy into a man of influence and rank. Barney Barnato, who began life with a trained
donkey, a London Jew, became at length the
South African Diamond King, and then all London paid homage to this despised son of a hated
race. Would money thus convert our despised
people into honorable citizens, give them kindly
recognition at the hands of their white neighbors,
and take from them the stigma which has so long
marked them with dishonor and shame? If so,
we can hope to secure even this coveted prize, and
claim like Barney Barnato the respect of mankind.

But if it is none of these things that doom us
to ostracism and degradation, as a people, I ask
finally is it our *color?* Alas, if it be this, we can
do nothing to remove the line of separation, unless it be to wait the slow process of amalgamation which, despite our efforts, the white people of
this country seem bound to consummate. If we
knew of any chemical preparation by which we
could change the color of our skins and straighten
the kinks in our hair, we might hope to bring
about the desired consummation at once, but
alas, there is no catholicon for this ill, no mystic
concoction in all the pharmacies of earth to work

this miracle of color. We must fold our hands in despair and submit to our fate with heavy hearts.

To be serious, however, I would plead with our white brothers not to despise us on account of our color. It is the inheritance we received from God, and it should be no mark of shame or dishonor. "Can the leopard change his spots or the Ethiopian his skin?" No disgrace can be attached to physical characteristics which are the result of heredity, and cannot be removed by any volition or effort. How cruel it is to visit upon the colored man contempt and dishonor because of the hue of his skin, or the curling peculiarity of his hair. Let him stand or fall upon his merit. Let him be respected if he is worthy. Let him be despised if he is unworthy.

We appeal to our white brothers to accord us simple justice. If we deserve good treatment give it to us, and do not consider the question of color any more than you would refuse kindness to a man because he is blind.

All we ask is a fair show in the struggle of life. We have nothing but the sentiment of kindness for our white brethren. Take us into your confidence, trust us with responsibility, and above all, show us cordial kindness. Thus will you link our people to you by the chains of love which nothing can break, and we will march hand in hand up the steep pathway of progress.